Mr. Kevin Cooke
19 Chestnut St Apt 4
Clinton, NY 13323

THE BLIZZARD

Previous books by Robert Bahr

Least of All Saints
The Virility Factor
Man With a Vision
Physical Fitness in Business and Industry
The Great Blizzard (for children seven to ten)

THE BLIZZARD

Robert Bahr

An Authors Guild Backinprint.com Edition

The Blizzard
All Rights Reserved © 1980, 2001 by Robert Bahr

No part of this book may be reproduced or transmitted in any form
or by any means, graphic, electronic, or mechanical, including photocopying,
recording, taping, or by any information storage or retrieval system,
without the permission in writing from the publisher.

AN AUTHORS GUILD BACKINPRINT.COM EDITION

Published by iUniverse.com, Inc.

For information address:
iUniverse.com, Inc.
5220 S 16th, Ste. 200
Lincoln, NE 68512
www.iuniverse.com

Originally published by Prentice Hall

ISBN: 0-595-15294-5

Printed in the United States of America

For Keith the Great

PREFACE

Every morning for two weeks during that January of 1977, we awakened to a temperature of thirteen degrees below zero. A few months earlier, our small family had moved from a city duplex to a hastily built woodland cabin in the mountains above Macungie, Pennsylvania. It had no insulation, no storm windows—only expensive electric heat and a cute, useless fireplace that permitted down drafts to shower the living room with glowing ashes and clouds of smoke.

That January, the indoor temperature never climbed above sixty-two degrees. We wore coats to dinner, slept fully dressed. Still, our electric bill quickly approached two thousand dollars.

Water pipes froze, and we had to collect drinking and cooking water from a stream behind the cabin.

At about the time Florida citrus crops were freezing and Buffalo was confronting its great blizzard, snow avalanched into that tiny stream, froze and forced the water over its banks, across ten feet of ice and into our basement window. While the water climbed the carpeted steps to the living room, we drove through blowing snowdrifts to the hardware store, bought a sump pump and set it up in two feet of basement water so cold that a skin of ice had formed across the surface. The pump held its own, and a day later we dug open the stream bed.

Each night we huddled around the television set to learn of the latest weather crises affecting other areas and people—particularly the citizens of western New York and Buffalo. Never in that city's history had a more severe winter been recorded; unequaled cold, winds and snowfall had paralyzed the entire area. On January 28, 1977, one of the worst blizzards on record struck the city.

But the crisis of that incomparable winter went far beyond western New York. From Milwaukee to Miami, a continuing stream of brutal Arctic wind created for millions of families their own individual dramas. Farmers lost thousands of dollars in crops; dairymen watched their cattle die. In Ohio, many endured subzero temperatures in unheated homes. Hundreds of thousands were laid off from work because of energy shortages. Stories like those dominated the headlines and the evening news broadcasts.

And we looked forward to those nightly reports with particular eagerness, to learn not of others' suffering but of their triumphs. In a way usually reserved for international conflicts like the Iranian crisis and wars, much of the nation felt a unity during that January of 1977. We had a common enemy, the winter, and we who struggled against an icy stream in the Macungie woods did battle with the same foe as those who fought in greater numbers on the streets of Buffalo. We got by in Macungie, and in Buffalo, and across the nation, because we helped each other through what was the most severe winter ever recorded in American history.

This book is about that winter, and in particular its effects upon Buffalo, New York's second largest city, the metropolis most brutally assaulted by the weather that year. In telling it, I've drawn upon several thousand pages of published material, most significantly the following:

—The October 1976 through February 1977 issues of the Buffalo *Evening News* and Buffalo *Courier-Express*, the city's two newspapers.

—*White Death*, by Erno Rossi. Half of Rossi's book deals with the blizzard's devastating effects in Canada, and makes for fascinating reading.

These and other printed sources appear in the bibliography.

But this book could not have been written on research done primarily in libraries. It's the product of literally hundreds of interviews with taxi drivers, bellboys, salespersons, parking lot attendants, passengers on the city's buses, pedestrians. It was through conversations with those many nameless people that the shape of that winter took form and the major themes gained prominence.

This book is not intended as an exhaustive account of the Buffalo blizzard—not half a million books could accomplish that, for every citizen stranded on area highways had his or her own story, many of them dramatic. The events related here are entirely true and verified in writing by the participants—but they are merely representative, not exhaustive. Lou Billittier was only one of scores who kept their restaurants open throughout the night of the blizzard; Bill Strobele's courageous walk was matched by several other policemen, firefighters and even private citizens. Those who live in these pages are symbolic of hundreds of thousands in cities, villages and the countryside of western New York who faced and overcame similar hardships.

Following are some of those who provided interviews, personal notes and official records:

The National Guard: Lt. Col. Gerald V. Harris; William Bellis; Lou Vallone; Warren Schrum, editor, *The Voice*.

Greater Buffalo International Airport: Richard F. Rebadow, general manager; Robert Stone, assistant manager; Sebastian Castro, superintendent of buildings; Stanley Kowalewski, custodian.

Delaware Park Labor Center: Al Nowiki, superintendent; Angelo Pintabowa; Mark Cvajkowlski; Mark DuMond.

Niagara Mohawk Company: William Abendshein, co-shift supervisor; Al Osborne, Bill Vogel, public relations; Mert Wagner, Joe Sullivan, Don Clark, troubleshooters; George Hilliker.

U.S. Weather Service, Buffalo: Don Wuersch, presently chief meteorologist in charge; Ben Kolker, deputy meteorologist; Richard Sheffield, Bill Hillig, Ed Reich, Dick Rausch.

Buffalo Police Department: Lt. John C. Brown; officers Paul Russi, Joe Weber, John O'Roark, George Smith; Lt. John C. Brown; dispatcher Bill Strobele.

City Hall: Les Foschio, former corporation counsel ("deputy mayor"); Leslie Greenbaum, former assistant corporation counsel; James Lindner, commissioner of streets and sanitation; Margaret Waggoner, secretary to James Lindner; others who prefer anonymity.

New York State Department of Transportation: Ed Janak, assistant regional highway maintenance engineer.

Buffalo Fire Department: Chief Jerry Sullivan, the alarm office.

Salvation Army: Ruth E. Allen; Major Bob Williams; Bob Harvey.

U.S. Army Corps of Engineers: Hank Vitale, emergency operations manager.

Others whose help is gratefully acknowledged include Woody Wardlow, managing editor of the Buffalo *Evening News;* Marian Dobiesz of the Microforms Room, Buffalo and Erie County Library; Joe Falzone of Whitney Place; Lou Billittier of Chef's Restaurant; Rose Ann Wagner of Emil's Inn; Paul Dengler; my secretary, Barbara Erich; my wife, colleague and friend, Alice Harrison Bahr.

Providing essential astronomical, atmospheric and climatic details were astronomer Val Gonzales, assistant director of the planetarium at the Franklin Institute in Philadelphia; A. James Wagner of the Climate Analysis Center in the World Weather Building, Washington, D.C.; and Elliot Abrams, vice president of Accu-Weather, Inc.

CONTENTS

Preface *v*
THE BLIZZARD
Part One *1*
Part Two *85*
Part Three *139*
Bibliography *182*

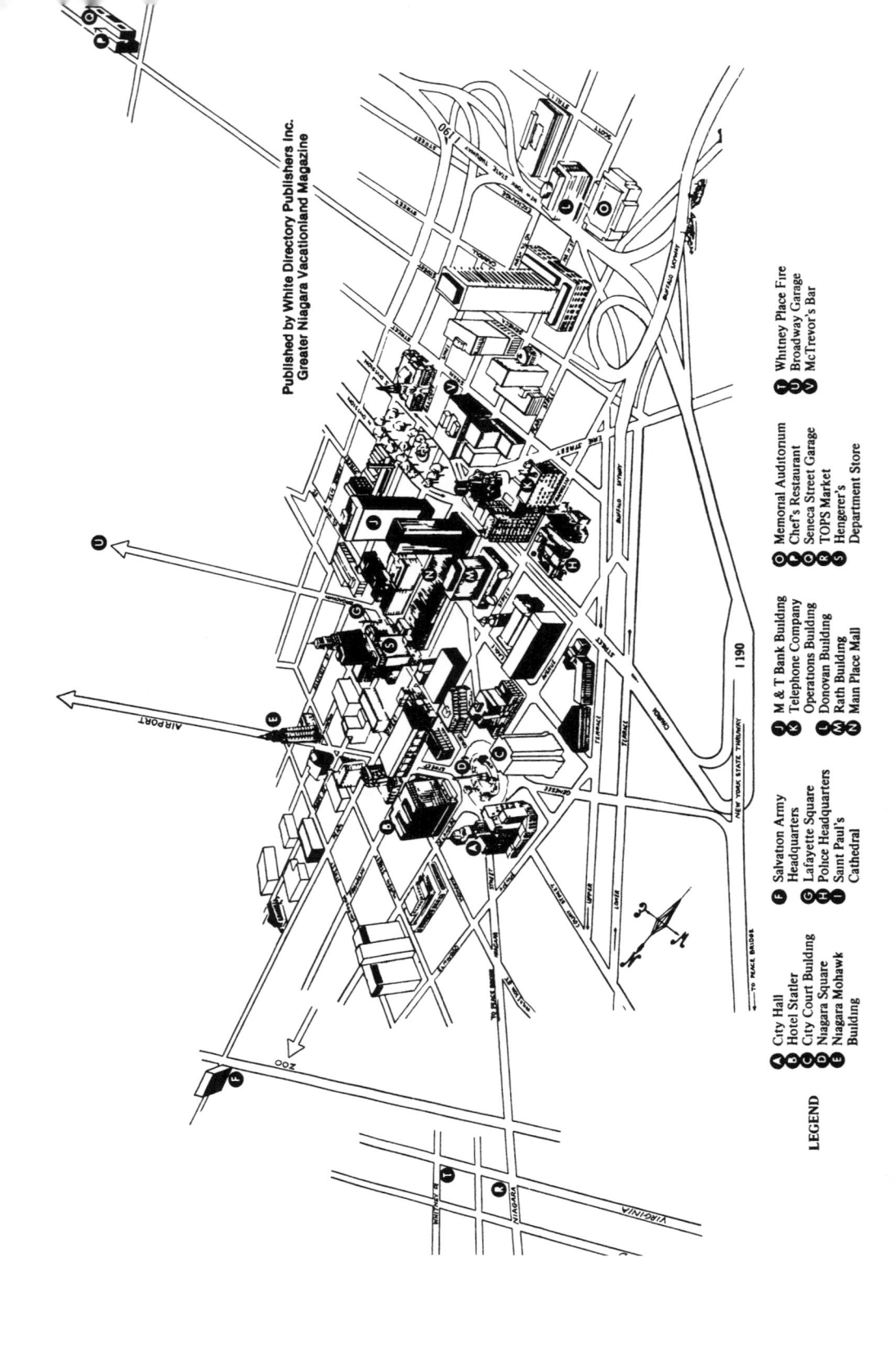

Published by White Directory Publishers Inc.
Greater Niagara Vacationland Magazine

LEGEND

- **A** City Hall
- **B** Hotel Statler
- **C** City Court Building
- **D** Niagara Square
- **E** Niagara Mohawk Building
- **F** Salvation Army Headquarters
- **G** Lafayette Square
- **H** Police Headquarters
- **I** Sant Paul's Cathedral
- **J** M & T Bank Building
- **K** Telephone Company Operations Building
- **L** Donovan Building
- **M** Rath Building
- **N** Main Place Mall
- **O** Memorial Auditorium
- **P** Chef's Restaurant
- **Q** Seneca Street Garage
- **R** TOPS Market
- **S** Hengerer's Department Store
- **T** Whitney Place Fire
- **U** Broadway Garage
- **V** McTrevor's Bar

PART 1

> 'Tis a noble and heroic thing, the wind!
> Who ever conquered it? In every fight
> it has the last and bitterest blow. . . .
> And yet, I say again, and swear it now,
> that there's something all glorious and
> gracious in the wind. —Ahab in MOBY DICK
> by Herman Melville

JANUARY 1977

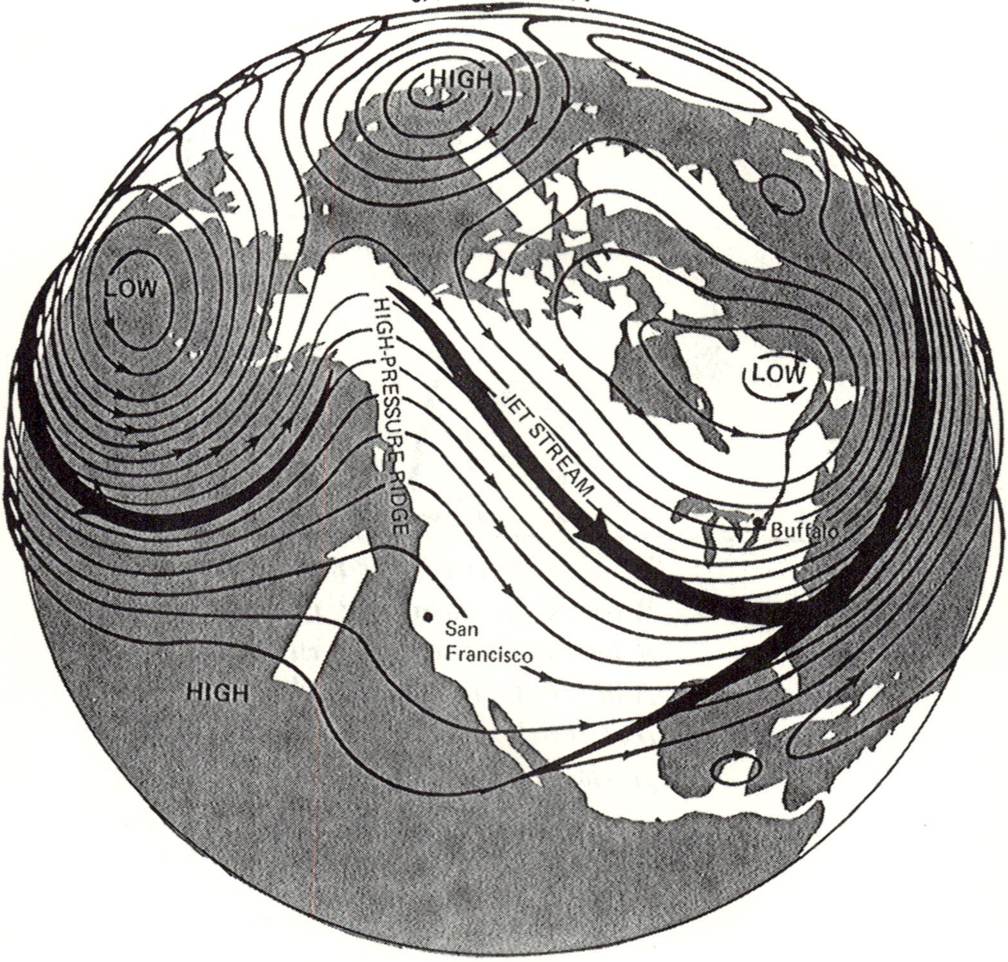

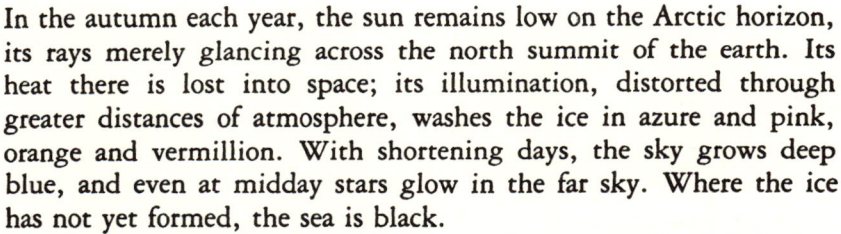

In the autumn each year, the sun remains low on the Arctic horizon, its rays merely glancing across the north summit of the earth. Its heat there is lost into space; its illumination, distorted through greater distances of atmosphere, washes the ice in azure and pink, orange and vermillion. With shortening days, the sky grows deep blue, and even at midday stars glow in the far sky. Where the ice has not yet formed, the sea is black.

With dusk on November 24, 1976, two months of night settled upon the Arctic. Yet the darkness was relative, for the sky over much of that five and a half million square miles of mostly frozen sea was clean and rare, and the stars in the north constellation cast brilliant reflections over the patches of water.

Moreover, a full moon appeared and drifted along the horizon for eighteen hours. Too low to illuminate the deep crags of the glaciers, those places remained in unbroken darkness. But it gleamed across all the desolate islands and sweeping treeless tundra, upon thousands of miles of surf breaking and freezing over rocky beaches. And across all the vast open space of the North—the floes, the plains of ice and dark patches of sea—the moonlight fell pure and cold. That night the sterile light swept the unbroken ice of the East Siberian Sea and the Greenland ice pack. Off the coast of Norway, it made radiant the soaring cliffs of glacial ice. Near Svalbard Island, an ice floe reflected the moon's rays against the belly of a solitary cloud. Thus, two moons of almost equal intensity brightened the island.

Near Victoria Island in the Canadian archipelago, a light breeze swept millions of ice crystals into the air. In the moonlight, they glittered like the dust of diamonds, showering the desolate land with opalescence.

White bears stood motionless on the ice, casting shadows, while ringed seals lingered near their breathing holes in the floes, and giant walruses, resting nearby, lifted unblinking eyes to survey the night for approaching bears.

The heat of the earth seeped from the ocean floor and raised the temperature of the frigid surrounding water a fraction of a degree. The slightly-warmed water, now lighter than its surroundings, lifted slowly toward the surface. Seals, huddling beneath the ice, their noses alone projecting through tiny breathing holes, might have felt the change.

Surface ice absorbed the heat and then gave it to the air, where again the upward motion of the lighter, less frigid currents lifted with ever-increasing speed through the cold atmosphere. The Arctic lost ever more heat, and, through the upward spiral, fresh breezes stirred.

Across all the Arctic the temperature continued to drop. The upper air, now profoundly cold and heavy, sank to spread like a great blanket over the surface of the earth. Layer upon layer, it accumulated, thickening, bulging into an inverted bowl, finally growing into an enormous mountain of dense and sluggish air, its invisible crest towering many miles above Everest, piercing the belly of the stratosphere.

On November 25, 1976, the center of this great mass was at 80 degrees latitude, north of the Laptev Sea. But it spilled south in every direction—from northern Siberia almost to Greenland, from the tiny islands above Norway to the Bering Strait. Bubbles breaking from the mass drifted toward the Aleutian Islands, Alaska and northern Canada. In the United States, they reached as far south as Buffalo.

The heavy, frigid polar air had settled upon one-fifth of the earth, just as it always has during the fall and winter. It was not an unusual season in the North, not until the great wind came.

2

At 10 P.M. the stores and offices in downtown Buffalo were closed. Light traffic moved along the main arteries to the suburbs, its sounds hushed by the snow blanketing the roads and piled in great banks along the curbs. On Main Street near Lafayette Square, where during the day the city was its busiest, neither cars nor pedestrians could be seen, only fine snowflakes gliding past a bobbing traffic light, to be dashed against the gaily colored lenses by a capricious gust.

Four blocks away, on Delaware Avenue, Paul Dengler, with collar raised against the freshly blowing snow, fumbled with the key to his little Hornet. Damn wind, he thought. Even the weatherman was never sure when it would appear, or from where, and in what measure of fury. Only one thing was certain this winter—the snow. It had begun falling late in October, and today, January 26, 1977, it was still snowing. On all but a handful of those intervening days, there'd been at least some precipitation.

Snow—lots of it—was a fact of life each winter to the 463,000 people of the city and the million and a half others who lived in the Buffalo metropolitan area. Although the state's second largest city, rich in culture and sophistication, its people boasted that theirs was the premier town of the Niagara Frontier—twenty miles to the north, beyond Kenmore, Tonawanda and Grand Island, was Niagara Falls, and beyond that, Lake Ontario and the Canadian wilderness. To the west the suburbs of Cheektowaga, Lancaster and Depew, then the hills and forests of the state of New York, and Rochester, eighty miles east. South of the city, more suburbs—Blasdell, Hamburg,

Orchard Park—and the Pennsylvania woodlands a hundred miles farther.

Only to the southwest was there neither suburb nor forest, for there, behind the City Hall, the hub of the city's center, lay Lake Erie.

In such geographical isolation, the hardy outpost spirit still thrived, and many considered the average annual snowfall of almost seven feet and winds that might reach forty miles an hour in any season to be assets. Coolness in summer, and opportunities for winter recreation were among the rewards.

But the winter of 1976–77 had been different. Even Paul Dengler, who loved the snow, had grown weary of it, and finally frustrated.

Bouncing over a small drift that had formed at its wheels, Dengler's Hornet lurched into Delaware Avenue and moved south toward the City Hall. New drifts were already building where, earlier in the day, plows had carved through them. Paul steered around the larger ones, throttled expertly through the others. He'd lived in the Buffalo area for twenty-five years, since his birth, had watched his father drive these snow-covered roads every year and had learned to drive them himself—it was a colossal nuisance.

By morning it would be worse than ever, he knew. These virtually empty streets would be crawling with thousands of autos again, all proceeding single file along the spokelike arteries to the hub of the wheel, the downtown—City Hall and Niagara Square. From the north, east and south the traffic would merge, bumper to bumper and congested for as far as anyone could see. In the spring, when the snow melted, these boulevards would be two and three lanes wide again, but now, clogged with abandoned cars and towering snowbanks, many were almost impassable.

From the west alone there would come no tangled confluence of blaring horns and coughing exhaust pipes. From that direction, behind City Hall, only the wind would rush, as always, howling summer and winter across the lake, the ten thousand square miles of Lake Erie.

Bearing to the right at Niagara Square, Paul drove along Delaware toward the lake, then turned left onto the lower terrace. A block south, he crossed Church Street and entered the Skyway heading south toward the suburb of Blasdell and home. It was almost 10:30.

Beside the lake, the snow was blowing furiously and Paul

worked to keep the Hornet steady. The highway seemed empty except for a single set of headlights reflecting in his mirror and the dual red glow of one car's taillights peering out of the snow ahead.

So dense was the snow now that the swirl outside the Hornet's warm interior seemed unreal. Across the divider, an occasional car passed on its way back to Buffalo, appearing suddenly out of the solitude, lingering, then vanishing like a magician's rabbit in a curtain of snow.

Except for those ever-fainter taillights ahead and the distant headlights behind, the snow quickly became visually impenetrable. Paul knew by the highway's contour that even now he was passing the Fuhrmann Boulevard eddy, the Coast Guard base and, at the farthest point, the lighthouse. On a clear night, that beacon could be seen on Lake Erie's Pennsylvania and Ohio shores. Yet now, a couple of thousand feet from it, he couldn't discern the faintest glow.

Nor could he detect any sign of the city behind him or traffic on Fuhrmann Boulevard, which swept in from the eddy to parallel the Skyway 100 feet below.

Following a momentary lull, a gust of great force struck the Hornet squarely, spraying the windshield with blinding snow and thrusting the car to the left. Paul swerved to the right, recovering. Quickly the windshield cleared and once more he could discern the taillights ahead. They grew closer.

Just don't stop, for God's sake, Paul thought.

Now the Skyway dipped to ground level and merged with Fuhrmann Boulevard. Here violent winds, funneled by the narrowing north and south shores of the lake, hurled across the east bank and the highway. The Hornet shuddered. With visibility at zero, Paul slowed almost to a stop.

The massive Freezer Queen factory was not more than a few hundred yards to Paul's right, between the highway and the lake. Yet he could see not a single light from its many windows. About three yards separated him from the creeping taillights ahead; yet for several seconds at a time they seemed to vanish. Even the headlights close behind him frequently disappeared from his mirror.

Paul felt the tension in his neck and arms, and shrugged to relieve it. He couldn't be more than a quarter of a mile from Tifft Street, he told himself, and just beyond that, the incline to Father Baker Bridge. From there, the road turned inland and the traveling would be much better. But the approach to the bridge was a sharp incline, no doubt covered with heavy drifts by now, and to traverse that stretch would require some speed and aggressive driving. The car ahead was moving much too slowly to make the incline. During the next few minutes it continued to lose speed, and finally, still a mile from the bridge, it stopped. Paul pumped his brakes to warn the car behind him. That car skidded perpendicular to the road, straightened and stopped.

He put the car in parking gear, turned the windshield wipers to low and leaned back, trying to resign himself to what could be a lengthy delay, perhaps even an hour, before they got the tow truck out to pull off the culprit causing the trouble. At least he had plenty of gas—the tank was almost three-quarters full.

If patience was the only alternative, he'd be patient—but in comfort. The temperature in the car was already beginning to fall, so he moved the heater to high. To shut out the eerie sound of the wind whooping around the car, the snow crystals scratching the windows, he turned on the radio and heard the last notes of a Barbra Streisand ballad. The weather forecast followed:

"A cold front crossing the central lakes this morning will bring snow to us sometime tonight. Several inches are likely over most of western New York. Then, as temperatures plummet tomorrow through Saturday, we'll have additional flurries and squalls. Temperatures Friday through the weekend will be mainly in the single numbers."

The cheerfulness of the announcer's voice irritated Paul. A cup of coffee at his elbow, no doubt. A cozy little studio. Why *not* be cheerful?

"Forecast for tonight, gusty southwest wind fifteen to thirty miles per hour becoming westerly twenty to thirty-five miles per hour later tonight. Considerable blowing and drifting snow. Chance of snow near one hundred percent tonight, ninety percent Thursday and seventy percent Thursday night."

They call that a weather forecast, Paul muttered to himself. Anybody with the brains to look out a window can see that.

He told himself he should have anticipated the problem—he knew that the Skyway and Fuhrmann Boulevard are closed as often as thirty times a year; in the summer it was the wind-driven rain; in the winter, the drifting snow. So common were these closings that the Buffalo police department had distributed plans for closing the Skyway at various points to all lake-area precincts. One such plan was no doubt already underway, and a police cruiser would soon guide them off the road. It would be a slow journey to Blasdell, to be sure, for traffic was heavy on South Park and the road was a battlefield of potholes. Still, had he taken that route in the beginning, he'd have been almost home by now.

*

The clock in the dashboard read 11 P.M. So he'd been stalled there, not the hour that it seemed, but only thirty minutes, yet in that brief time the weather had changed ominously. No longer did the wind appear in sudden squalls, then vanish. Now it drove a continuing barrage of snow against the car, the roar of it overwhelming the radio's music, its impact swaying the Hornet on its springs. Melting and refreezing snow had already formed a solid crust of ice on the car's lakeside windows, and the ice now encroached upon the windshield. With the blades frozen, the wipers continued their ineffective clattering across the windshield, while the moisture from Paul's breath condensed as frost on the inside of the glass, making it impossible to see even the taillights ahead. Using the side of his gloved hand, Paul scraped the frost away.

Another gust shook the car, and a flutter of fine snow sprayed through invisible passages and hung suspended for a moment in the air inside. Paul felt the surge of coldness around his ankles, a palpable drop in temperature even with the heater working full force. For the first time that night he felt fear.

From the driver's-side window he could see the drift of snow against the medial rail, already blocking half the outside lane. Certainly drifts were also building against the lake-side of the Hornet, slowly burying him.

He sat for what seemed a very long time, refusing to acknowledge the mere forty-five minutes the dashboard clock indicated had passed. He told time now by the gas gauge—it indicated less than half full—and by the continuous scrape of the wipers, now utterly useless. Finally he shut them off. He also dimmed the headlights to save power, and when the announcer began to repeat the weather forecast, he shut off the radio, too. The whole universe consisted of the glowing dashboard, the howl of wind, the impenetrable ice and the driving snow, visible only through a small space on the window to his left.

As he sat there shivering he considered the frightening possibility that help might not ever come. In such a driving squall, no one might even see the few cars stranded on this lonely stretch of

Skyway. No doubt by now the entrances had all been closed, and no one would travel it until after the snow stopped. Then the plows would come through and find—what?

He could not sit there helplessly, waiting to be frozen to death. Turning his collar up, he opened the door and stepped into the snow.

The wind threw him back against the door. The cold numbed his face and pierced his heavy winter clothing. His glasses were almost torn from his face. Still, leaning against the car, he took several steps forward. Out of the whiteness appeared the same set of taillights he'd followed earlier. Squinting through the driving snow, he saw more red lights, several pairs. So there were more than just the two of them. A first-class tie-up, no doubt. Probably an accident.

Perhaps he could get help. Someone might be seriously hurt in one of those cars. If he could at least reach a telephone, he could call the police.

But it was an absurd idea, he knew. The relative warmth of his glasses had already melted some snow, and the water had frozen, distorting his vision.

Even with his gloves on, his fingers ached with the cold. So did his feet, and his face was utterly numb. He might manage ten steps or twenty, but the wind would blow him off course, his vision would be so impaired that he'd lose his direction and wander blindly for—what, ten minutes? Half an hour? The temperature was about ten degrees, the windchill factor minus thirty. Here, on the outskirts of the second largest city in New York, he could freeze to death, and it would happen in a matter of minutes, certainly before midnight. It seemed incredible, even ridiculous, that he could be frozen to death by a mere freak lake squall, a momentary aberration of nature, while still within the boundaries of a great city. It was almost an insult. Yet it was true.

He started back to the car, kicking through a foot and a half of fresh snow. His fingers were at first too numb to depress the lock in the door, then he discovered that the lock itself had frozen. Pounding it with his fist, he broke the ice loose and a moment later slammed the door shut behind him.

For an hour, Paul huddled behind the steering wheel shivering, his hands and feet aching with the cold, his face void of all feeling.

He reached for the rear-view mirror and twisted it so that he could see the reflection of his face. Ice crystals clung to his eyebrows, and unmelted snow gave him the appearance of the hoary aged. It occurred to him with no particular concern as he stared into the reflection of glazed eyes that he was already frozen, already dead.

He dropped his vision to the gas gauge. The needle was approaching empty. He'd been sitting there forever, the engine purring casually toward extinction.

All at once he stopped shivering. Perhaps the car heater was winning the battle against the wind after all. He felt warmer now, even comfortable, although sapped of energy and sleepy. Just as well, he thought, there's nothing for it but to be patient. Might as well sleep. Might just as well.

He laid his arms across the steering wheel and rested his head on them. His eyelids fluttered shut. They'll freeze closed like that, he thought, the lashes against the socket, the tears sealing them solid. Freeze probably, he thought. Not enough gas to suffocate.

3

These are the origins of the great winds: the earth's spinning; the sun's heat. Both reach extremes at the equator, and it is there, in the blister of rising air, the lazy undulations of convection, that the great winds are born.

The deserts and seas of that torrid zone may seem as still as death, but in fact all, including the air, are hurtling at a thousand miles an hour through the endless cycle of days and nights.

Rising high into the troposphere, the layer of atmosphere nearest the earth, the warm air spills from the equatorial zone to the north and south. To the north, it passes above Jacksonville and New Orleans, Cairo and Shanghai, where the earth's circumference is half that of the equator, its rotation only 500 miles an hour. Yet, seven miles above the earth at that latitude, the equatorial air, somewhat cooled now in the temperate climate, hurls northward at a speed only slightly less than that of the equator. That is the beginning.

A virtual infinity of factors governs the wind's direction: towering mountains, breathless deserts, the swirling tides of hot air through cold, the varying capacity of the earth's surface to reflect the sun's heat back into the atmosphere. By such phenomena is the direction of the wind dictated.

Each moment the energy equivalent of seven million atomic bombs is expended driving the winds.

*

The west wind does not touch the earth. Yet, as the sparrow caught in the wake of an airliner is hurled to instant destruction, so the "upper level westerlies" determine man's destiny. Their domain is the stratosphere where dwell the wispy ice of the cirrus, the occasional crest of a great, stormy cumulus. On this rarefied and seemingly empty space 30,000 to 45,000 feet above the seas, the great winds rush eternally from west to east around the planet.

Season upon season the westerlies flow, tearing a swath 1,000 miles wide and several thousand feet deep through the surrounding air. And the core of that atmospheric river, the jet stream, sometimes rages at speeds of 300 miles an hour.

*

During the summer, the sun warms the water of the Pacific Ocean and the water in turn passes its moist heat into the languid air. Rising into the tow of the westerlies, this air sweeps across thousands of miles of ocean, and in the autumn, fully saturated, it rolls across the western states of America. There, cooled by the earth, it drops its moisture in great sheets of rain. Parched deserts grow green and colorful. Hot pebbles of the riverbeds steam and tumble in the downpour. Brooks and lakes are reborn and, inland, cattle moan and drink.

But in the summer of 1976, these predictable events did not occur. A vast basin of unseasonably cold water lay motionless in the North Pacific, its core lingering from the previous winter when it was dragged south beneath the sweeping current of the Arctic Ocean. Over all that great expanse of sea one phenomenon followed another to prevent the water's warming. Heavy cloud cover blocked the sun's radiation. Continual strong winds carried away what little heat had gathered on the water's surface. Thus, from the south coast of Alaska to northern California, from the Aleutians almost to Hawaii, the North Pacific sea temperatures fell to an all-time summer low.

Eventually, the surface winds ceased. The water chilled the stagnant air, and the cooled atmosphere grew heavy upon the water. Throughout the summer its pressure grew greater, the sprawling mass finally dominating much of the North Pacific. Like a dome, it pushed ever higher, until it exceeded even the level of the westerlies.

For all their power, those great winds could not penetrate the mass. They swerved from the mountain of air, ricocheting southward, where another unlikely phenomenon had developed.

While the water of the North Pacific was setting low-temperature records, another body of Pacific water a few hundred miles south had reached temperatures dramatically above normal. This contrasting drift extended from about the 180th meridian to the California coast at latitudes from 25 to 35 degrees. The air over that water grew hot and light, expanding. But the expansion was channeled, for the dense cold air blocked it to the northwest, and the Coast Range and Cascades and Sierra Nevada offered some resistance to the east. Moreover, seasonal high pressure along the coast created an invisible but impenetrable ridge along the entire coast.

Thus, the warm air expanded leisurely northward toward Alaska, forming a moist low-pressure trough west of California and parallel to the coast.

It was into the trough that the westerlies, rebounding from the Pacific high-pressure mass, swooped. The warm, wet air in its tow never reached inland to shower the western states, but was tugged northward. Alaska, usually shivering under the polar cold-air mass by mid-autumn, awakened to balmy temperatures in the forties, and frequent rain showers.

Ever northward the westerlies surged, across Anchorage, Fairbanks, the frozen tundra banking Mackenzie Bay, the ice-covered Beaufort Sea. There, high over the Arctic, the wind plunged against that sprawling mass of dense, frigid air hovering over the north summit. The wind surged upward to leap the crest of polar air, but there seemed no end to its height. Spiraling higher and higher, the rising edge of the west wind grew cold and heavy and became a ceiling through which its lower currents could not penetrate.

A battle line formed, a front, where the gradient in temperatures between the polar mass and the westerlies was most profound. Along that front, cataclysmic storms raged, the warm air jetting upward, the cold plunging in far-reaching swirls of enormous force. Snow whipped the icy sea to great fury and the rare pole lightning ruptured the sky.

For all that, the polar mass did not surrender. Rather, the wind swerved, as it had days earlier around the other high-pressure mass in the North Pacific. Now sapped of its heat, towing in its wake bubbles of ground-level Arctic air, it surged south over Victoria Island and the Northwest Territories. Temperatures plunged in Saskatchewan and Manitoba, from the eastern foothills of the Rockies to Hudson Bay.

For many weeks the pattern continued, the west wind coiling like a snake from the North Pacific south to the trough, then north to the Arctic and rebounding south again across North America. Upon reaching Topeka and St. Louis, the wind did not swerve from its southern course to pursue its traditional journey east to Washington, D.C., and the Atlantic, but continued beyond Tulsa and Dallas, looping north again only upon reaching the Gulf.

Out of the west wind fell snow and unprecedented cold.

In the Northeast, frigid temperatures exhausted the fuel supply. In Michigan, automobile plants closed to conserve energy, and 50,000 workers were laid off. The National Guard was called out to deliver heating oil, food and medicine to snowbound families in western counties.

As the winter progressed, Chicago reached a record snowfall of seven feet. From Philadelphia to Peoria, January 1977 was the coldest month ever recorded. A blizzard in Indiana stranded 3,500 cars and trucks on Interstate 65. Evansville hit a temperature of minus 21 degrees. In Dunkirk, three-fourths of the labor force were put out of work when businesses and factories ran out of heating fuel.

Missouri was buried under 23.9 inches of snow, more than double the old record. The Huntsville, Alabama, Civil Defense brought drinking water to many residents, for water pipes all over the city burst when temperatures plummeted from the typical 63 degrees to minus 1 and remained below 26 for more than five weeks.

Snow fell farther and farther south, from Texas through the Carolinas and Florida. Houston recorded the coldest winter in history. Tomatoes there froze in the field. Jackson, Mississippi, reached six degrees above zero.

Dayton, Ohio, set a new low-temperature record of minus 21 degrees, with temperatures day after day for months averaging seventeen degrees colder than normal. Cincinnati was even colder, the Ohio River there freezing over completely. Natural gas stores were virtually exhausted. The governor declared an emergency, and only federal intervention prevented mass freezing deaths.

In northeastern Pennsylvania, the Monongahela River froze solid, immobilizing barges laden with thousands of tons of coal. The people of Fayette County, where oil and kerosene stores were already exhausted and the area was paralyzed by minus-20 and minus-30 degree temperatures, watched in terror the deathly encroachment of the cold. In the towns of Unionville and Connellsville, where water mains are buried four to five feet below the earth to prevent freezing, 300 of them burst. A crew of thirty-five men worked sixteen-hour shifts for weeks digging through the frozen ground to repair them.

A few hundred miles south, the Chesapeake Bay froze and seven thousand fishermen lost a total of ten million dollars in income. Farther south, Baltimore Harbor, too, was sealed with an eight-inch cap of ice that crushed boats and popped the caulking from their hulls. One after another they sank.

A rush-hour snowstorm in Washington, D.C., caused a traffic tie-up that didn't dissolve until midnight.

During January, it snowed in Miami and Palm Beach. Pensacola had a record low temperature of 10 degrees. Florida's citrus growers kept crews busy night after night stoking bonfires in the groves to combat the crop-killing mid-teens temperatures. Still authorities continued to predict a 900-million-dollar loss in citrus, vegetable and tourist money.

On January 24, the Buffalo *Courier-Express* published this editorial:

> It has been a trying winter for western New Yorkers, but there is some consolation in reading the weather reports from across the nation—snow in Florida, 25 degrees below zero in Cincinnati and an "energy emergency" declared in Minnesota, traffic virtually halted on the ice-clogged Mississippi. Reports are the same all over.
>
> Difficult as it has been, Buffalonians can find some solace in reading about folks shoveling snow in Pensacola, in bearing sleet storms in Tampa, and buried under four inches of snow in Tulsa, Oklahoma. We are not alone. The forecast from the official weather service is snow today, stretching all the way from the southwest to the Great Lakes and the northeast. Showers are predicted for Florida, changing to rain and snow in the southern coastal states.

That was on January 24. Two days later, shortly after midnight, snow half-buried Paul Dengler's Hornet on the Buffalo Skyway as he slumped, unconscious and freezing, across the steering wheel.

4

In the northwest corner of the second floor at the Buffalo Police Headquarters a few blocks from City Hall, one of the most sophisticated police dispatch systems in the country operates. Twenty-four hours a day a staff of nine complaint writers stands ready to answer emergency calls from all over the county, including Buffalo, to record every complaint immediately on a 3" x 6" yellow card, insert it into a time-punch clock and drop it onto a conveyor belt that speeds the card to a dispatcher's desk in an adjoining room. The whole process can be accomplished in twenty seconds.

    Just before midnight on January 26, Bill Strobele took his position at the dispatcher's desk and skimmed the solitary card awaiting him. He turned to the illuminated map of the city on the far wall. On it were tiny lights representing the patrol cars then cruising the city, red indicating those on call, green the ones available for duty. Bill Strobele stepped on a pedal near his foot and spoke into the microphone, his voice a soft monotone:

    "Car thirteen-N, there's a stranded motorist under the viaduct on Elmwood. That's between Hertel and Amherst."

    "Roger," came the reply.

    Bill inserted the yellow card in a time clock to record the time the call was sent and filed it in a box near his right elbow. When the officers in Car 13-N reported the matter resolved, the card would be punched yet a third time, filed and eventually microfilmed.

    Bill continued to process new cards almost mechanically while, a few feet from his head, fire department and medical emergency radio systems blared. When he had a free moment, he skimmed through the calls in progress. Three had to do with the snow. A man was stranded on Roanoke Parkway. Two girls were snowbound in a green station wagon on Bailey and Seneca, a few blocks from headquarters.

And in the southbound lane of the Skyway, on the approach to Father Baker Bridge, two cars had spun out of control, blocking the road.

"What's the condition of Fuhrmann and the Skyway?" Bill asked an officer who'd just come off duty.

"Blowing like hell."

According to reports, the bridge had been blocked since 11:27. It was now five after midnight. Bill depressed the pedal, turning on the microphone.

"Attention all western precincts. Precincts three, seven, nine, ten, fifteen and motorcycle division. We're putting Plan One into effect immediately. Plan One—close the Skyway."

With that, six patrol cars started toward the lakefront. One barricaded the Church Street ramp near City Hall, two blocks from Police Headquarters. Another proceeded to the New York Thruway entrance. A car from Precinct 7 set up lights and barricades on Louisiana Street, then blocked the Southeast Service Drive.

In South Buffalo, officers Duane Bonamici and Joe Weber in car 627 were pulling away from Precinct 15, the South Park Station, when Bill Strobele's voice reached them.

They immediately headed north along South Park to the intersection with Tifft, then left toward the lake. There was no traffic in that direction, and soon the houses gave way to desolate flatlands and the shadow of an occasional factory. Here the wind gusted fiercely between the cruiser and the towering snowbanks.

A quarter of a mile from the lake, Joe Weber pointed to the left. Now and again there would occur a momentary ceasing of the wind, and in that instant the falling snow would take on the texture of a bolt of fine lace. Then the officers could recognize the distant glow of lights along Father Baker Bridge to the south. They were approaching the Skyway.

According to Plan One, the officers in car 627 had two responsibilities: to block the Tifft Street entrance to the northbound lanes of the Skyway, and to prevent cars that exited from the northbound lanes from turning right, toward the lake. Although there were some factories along Fuhrmann Boulevard, which bordered the

18

lake, Plan One assumed that road had already been blown shut. No doubt the middle shift from the factories would be stranded for a few hours, and the midnight shift simply wouldn't get in. But at least no one would spend the night shivering in a snow pile. Another cruiser from the fifteenth precinct would soon be taking its position on the west side of the Skyway underpass. Officers George Smith and John O'Roark would prevent the few who had managed to leave the factories from entering the Skyway's south lanes and becoming involved in a possible tie-up at Father Baker Bridge. Instead, Smith and O'Roark would direct traffic along Tifft Street to South Park. And they'd help keep motorists off of Fuhrmann Boulevard.

Bonamici and Weber had just set up the barricades and blinking lights at the Skyway entrance when they saw the snow-muffled glow of headlights approaching on the northbound exit ramp. Breaking out of the storm, the car barreled toward them, then slid to a stop. It was a Volkswagen Beetle, with a young woman at the wheel. She cranked down the window.

"Good thing you're here!" she shouted.

"You need help?"

"Not me—you kidding? *They* need help." Over the roaring wind, she yelled that dozens of cars were stranded in the southbound lane. Traffic was stalled all the way to Father Baker Bridge and halfway back to Buffalo.

"They're probably all frozen to death by now!" she exclaimed cheerfully, throwing the Volkswagen into gear.

"How did *you* get through?" Joe Weber asked. But the car puttered off into the blinding snow.

Pulling their scarves tight and grabbing flashlights, Bonamici and Weber left the car and trudged through the knee-deep drifts of the northbound entrance ramp. From across the lake the wind howled at thirty-five to forty miles per hour, whipping the snow with such force that it stung the officers' faces and brought tears to their eyes.

Approaching the Skyway, they saw the diffused glow of many headlights along the road from the city. The snow blurred the distant ones into a faint ribbon of light, but the nearer ones took on the appearance of moons shimmering through fog.

To the left, the tie-up continued toward Father Baker Bridge, the rows of taillights growing into a single scratch of red which quickly vanished in the swirling snow.

Joe Weber cupped his hands and yelled to Bonamici, "Those

19

cars aren't going anywhere tonight." Although they could see clearly only the two nearest vehicles, both were half buried in snow.

Leaning into the wind, the officers made their way to the medial rail, climbed over it and approached the first car, a new Oldsmobile. Bonamici pounded on the side window. The face of a man in his early thirties appeared behind the glass.

"You all right?"

"I guess so."

"Warm enough?"

"The heater's doing all right, but I'm running low on gas. Look, I'm Jeff Hensey, the attorney, and—"

"Turn off your headlights—it'll save a little energy. And don't fall asleep. We'll get you moving don't worry."

The two proceeded north through the drifts, checking every tailpipe to be sure it wasn't blocked, stumbling through the most violent gusts, pounding on frozen windshields, car roofs, doors.

A car full of teenagers had run out of gas and the battery was dead; the group had kept warm huddling together, complaining only that the radio wasn't operating.

A grandmother in a fur coat sat shivering in a small foreign car. The officers kicked the snow away from the door and led her to the vehicle behind hers, a new Cadillac.

It appeared that the line would be endless. In some areas, where drivers had attempted to pass stalled vehicles, they, too, had bogged down, thus blocking the outside lane. Other cars had skidded sideways, completely obstructing the road.

After twenty minutes, the officers approached the last set of headlights.

"Well, that's it," shouted Weber. "I counted about seventy-five of 'em—can you believe it?"

"Look," yelled Bonamici, "You go back and call for K-9 vans, whatever they can send—we gotta get these people off here." He pointed along the highway toward Buffalo. "There could be more out there. I'm gonna take a look."

Back in the cruiser, Weber called Bill Strobele, the dispatcher. Thirty seconds later, Strobele had two K-9 vans headed toward Tifft and the Skyway. Then he called the fire department and requested their personnel carrier. It would hold twenty-two people.

Officers George Smith and John O'Roark, stationed at the west side of the Skyway on Tifft Street, learned of the traffic tie-up a hundred feet above them through Weber's call to Strobele.

"Where you gonna put 'em once you get 'em in the vans?" Smith asked.

"Here, I guess," Strobele said.

"It's too far—we'll be driving back and forth all night. Let's see what I can do."

With the roadblocks in place, Smith and O'Roark headed back toward South Park. A few minutes later, they stopped at 1885 South Park, the Rectory of Holy Family Church, and Smith roused the pastor, Father Joseph Fiore. Minutes later, while Officers Smith and O'Roark drove back to the Skyway, Father Fiore struggled across the parking lot to the church school building to get some cookies and hot chocolate, and brought them to the church's basement kitchen. He turned on the lights and heat.

Officer Duane Bonamici had hiked not more than a few hundred feet when, three yards ahead, he came upon two more cars. The driver of the first indicated that he was bored, but comfortable. His heater was working and he still had plenty of gas. The second car was a green Hornet. The headlights were off, and the only engine Bonamici heard from that direction belonged to a truck, well behind the car. It appeared that the Hornet had been abandoned for some time—a thick layer of ice already covered the hood. Condensation inside the car had iced the windows, preventing Bonamici from seeing into the car.

He tried the door. It seemed to be locked, but he wasn't certain. He stooped down, his nose practically touching the window, and peered through a fracture in the frost pattern. It was too dark—he could see nothing. He placed his flashlight against the ice of the windshield, and the car's interior brightened. A young man lay slumped across the steering wheel.

"Hey, open the door!" Bonamici shouted, tugging futilely at the latch.

With both fists he pounded on the car's roof.

"Come on—come on, wake up, man!" he yelled. Through the crack in the frost he saw the man stir, the lids slowly rising to reveal vacant eyes. Bonamici flashed the light through the windshield again.

"Wake up!" he shouted. "Man, you're *freezing to death*!"

The eyelids drooped again, and Bonamici pounded the roof harder than before. The head snapped back and moved from side to side, the eyes opening wider.

"Listen, kid, open the door. You hear me? Open the door!"

Paul Dengler stared at the side window and the eyeball peering through the tiny crack in the frostline. He heard the voice again and again, harsh and intrusive, and although it seemed to make no sense, he finally reached for the door handle, tugging it halfheartedly, then harder, and finally with both hands and all his strength. With shattering of ice the door flew open and the handle ripped from Paul Dengler's grip.

"Come on," yelled Bonamici. "There's a truck back there someplace and we're gonna get you in it." But Dengler merely stared at him absently. The officer lifted him to his feet in the snow.

"Put your arm around my neck," he shouted, leading Dengler forward.

"Brought you some company," the officer yelled when Charles Zerrille threw open the door of his tractor-trailer cab.

"He looks in bad shape," Zerrille said, pulling Dengler inside.

"Help's coming," Bonamici said. He slammed the door and started back to Joe Weber and the cruiser.

By then, George Smith and John O'Roark were already leading people from the Skyway to their patrol car and driving them to Holy Family Church. Later, when the K-9 vans and the fire department transport vehicle arrived, they led them to the vehicles by the scores, instructing them to form human chains to prevent anyone from wandering off in the wrong direction and perishing.

*

On the second floor of police headquarters, Bill Strobele continued to dispatch complaints. Most of them were related to the snow.

*

At 1:12 A M. James Heidt, a police tow-truck driver sent to remove a stranded car from Father Baker Bridge, called in to explain the immediate cause of the Skyway tie-up: A tractor trailer had jackknifed on the incline to the bridge. Strobele sent car 7 to investigate, but there was nothing to be done except to rescue the stranded. Even the tow trucks would be of little use until the southbound lanes could be plowed clear.

1:35 A M—a car abandoned at 29 Josee was blocking the street.

1:57 A M.—a stranded motorist on Bailey.

2:18 A.M.—traffic jam under viaduct at Bailey and Dinginin.

3:00 A.M.—patrol car 12 reported it still had two miles of stranded drivers to evacuate.

Ten minutes later, a yellow card told Bill Strobele that ten motorists were stranded at 300 Louisiana Street. A New York Thruway employee had discovered them on his way to work.

By 3:50 A M an officer with the K-9 vans reported they had one mile to go. Two hours later, an executive at the Freezer Queen factory complained that hundreds of workers were marooned at the plant.

*

On the first floor of police headquarters, directly below the dispatch room, more than a hundred people milled about. Some talked with animation. Others congregated near the coffee urn. In one corner, Paul Dengler huddled alone, shivering, hoping not to spill the cup of coffee he clutched in both hands. A reporter questioned him. It was good to be alive, he said, but he didn't believe he'd ever be warm again.

At the opposite end of the room, attorney Jeff Hensey stood flushed with anger. He had called his wife to explain the delay, then four service stations to request a tow truck. None was open.

By 5:00 A M. the last motorists had been evacuated from the Skyway. Joe Weber, Duane Bonamici, George Smith, John O'Roark and many other officers had fought the wind and snow for almost five hours, their scarves frozen at their necks, ice clinging to their eyebrows. Their breath condensed as ice on their cheeks, and their hands were crippled with pain.

Yet as daylight diffused over the lake Thursday morning and the snow decreased to flurries, it seemed that the raging storm of the night could not have happened. Even the temperature was rising, and the sky was growing bright behind the clouds. The Skyway lay in silence, only the gleam of a windswept windshield or a flash of chrome giving evidence that the 140 white mounds convoluting along that five miles were, in fact, buried automobiles.

5

Although it was only 5:00 A M , James Lindner was driving to work He'd been awake for an hour, had monitored the police radio at home and knew all about Fuhrmann Boulevard, the Skyway and the rest of the city. Even in the car, he listened to Bill Strobele's voice. It was an exercise in masochism: James Lindner, Commissioner of Street Sanitation for the city of Buffalo, was the man responsible for unclogging the mess.

It had been a hell of a winter—nothing like it in Lindner's experience. As early as October, the icy winds had begun pummeling Buffalo. The temperature of the lake dropped to 48 degrees, lowest for October since 1928. A foot of snow fell that month, wet and heavy, snapping tree limbs and power lines. On the twenty-first, the temperature reached a record low for the date—23 degrees. Two days later, the high winds tipped a barge in the lake, dumping more than a thousand tons of stones into the north end of Buffalo Harbor. It was the city's second-coldest October in half a century.

Well, the weather does that, throws you a curve now and then. You can handle it. A little slow gearing up, maybe—who expects a foot of snow in October? You get the plows moving, and salt spreaders. No insurmountable problem.

But the stuff didn't want to melt, and when it did, it froze again and was treacherous. November's low temperatures broke an 1880 record. And on November 28, four days after the long night fell in the Arctic, the city encountered the season's first major storm. Snow began falling late that night, continuing during the early hours of the twenty-ninth, paralyzing rush-hour traffic. Two feet of snow on the city streets in little more than a day. By the end of November, the Lake Erie temperature had dropped to 38 degrees.

December's first storm started on the third and continued sporadically through the ninth. Winds reached fifty-five miles per hour. Six people died because of the storm. It snowed again on December 23, and again from the twenty-sixth to the twenty-ninth to set a new monthly snowfall record of 60.7 inches. It was also the fifth coldest December on record, with an average temperature of 22 degrees.

By then, the city had been clobbered with more than 92 inches of snow—13 inches above the *annual* average. Those who enjoyed doing such things predicted that, by the end of February, the 126.4 inch record set in 1909–10 would topple.

And still the snow continued—two inches on the first of January, three on the second, four and a half on the seventh—and on the tenth, a car-burying storm of thirteen inches. Almost four inches on the fifteenth, seven on the seventeenth. The month was almost gone and there'd been not one day without at least flurries.

The snow itself amounted to 50 percent of James Lindner's problems. The rest were caused by the unyielding cold. Christmas had been the last day above freezing in Buffalo. In fact, on Tuesday, the twenty-fifth, with thirty-one days of cold, the 1901 record for a period of subfreezing temperatures fell. If the weather forecasts for the next four days held accurate, this January would be the first in 107 years in which the temperature did not once rise above freezing. And it would be the coldest January in history, with the temperature averaging somewhere between 13 and 15 degrees for the entire month.

None of the snow melted. The city's plows pushed it aside, piled it in banks that towered ever higher and wider. In fact, so high were the snowbanks that Niagara Mohawk Power Company had issued a warning that in some neighborhoods the snow was reaching dangerously close to overhead electric wires.

At worst, furious winds drove the snow crystals into granite-like drifts against which the plows were impotent.

On the nineteenth, the Buffalo *Evening News* editorialized "We have lived through rough winters before, but this is getting ridiculous. Even the hardiest of us are ready to say uncle with chattering teeth through blue lips."

Driving to work that Thursday morning, Lindner admitted to himself that the battle to open the city's streets was all but lost. Earlier in the week, he'd made an official estimate that one in every five cars in the city was either abandoned or illegally parked. Drivers complained that they had nowhere to put their cars, since snowbanks filled the parking spaces, but Lindner, cursing and pounding the desk in his City Hall office, bellowed that the spaces could not be cleaned until the public moved the cars.

Eventually, most of the city's side streets became impassable. Thousands of residents protested. A few threatened violence. Only a handful moved their cars to private parking facilities.

That was just one of Lindner's problems. A few days earlier, he'd told the press that, of the $100,000 he'd allotted for salt for the entire winter, he'd already spent $225,000.

Yet, until last night, Lindner had felt he'd had a fighting chance. On Tuesday, he'd gotten all the major streets open—Elmwood, Delaware and Main to the north and south, Seneca and Swan east and west, Genesee northeast, Niagara northwest. Even Fuhrmann Boulevard and the Skyway had been cleared.

The politicians had come to his rescue. Two city council members—Herbert Bellamy and Patricia Gallivan—had demanded mass towing and ticketing to get cars off the streets, and in an editorial on the twenty-fifth the *Courier-Express* jumped on the bandwagon:

> We have had bad winter snows before, and heavy accumulations. What is lacking in this crisis, perhaps, is a feeling that has sometimes existed in the past of everyone pulling together in a systematic battle against the elements. With a stronger show of leadership at City Hall, and better cooperation of all concerned, an all-out effort can be mounted to get this difficult job done within the next few days.

By Tuesday morning, the "Snow Blitz," as the press had dubbed it, was in full swing. Mayor Stanley Makowski pleaded with the public on Monday to remove cars from streets scheduled for plowing and warned that there would be mass ticketing and towing. He did so under political pressure, for Stanley Makowski would rather have been executed than hurt anyone's feelings. His opponents often said he'd have made an ideal priest. Nonetheless, 500 cars were tagged and 80 towed on Tuesday. Lindner would have towed twice as many, but the city owned just seven old tow trucks, and all but two had broken down. Nor would others be purchased, for although New York City had cornered the national publicity regarding municipal bankruptcies that season, Buffalo, too, was in severe economic difficulty.

The Commissioner of Streets had kept in close touch with Joseph Tomasula, his chief of Radio Communications. Tuesday morning Tomasula reported, "The people generally aren't responding." The department had posted signs announcing the plowing, and had sent men with bullhorns along the streets several times urging people to remove their cars.

"Why, I even had the men write down license-plate numbers," Tomasulo complained. "We ran 'em through the computer and phoned the owners—and they *still* didn't move the cars."

In a few neighborhoods, a single illegally parked car kept the plows idle for half a day.

Lindner had seen the problems himself on some of the side streets east of Niagara. Three drivers had abandoned cars in the middle of Normal Avenue, although plowed and empty parking lots bordered both sides of the street. A few blocks away, a driver cut in front of a moving plow in order to park in the street in front of it.

Yet, in spite of such difficulties, Lindner had estimated that thirty-five miles of streets had been cleared by Tuesday night.

Wednesday, things had gone even better. Some buses were still being rerouted because of blocked streets, and cars were still stalling in traffic and being abandoned there. But the newspapers published the plowing schedule, and Lindner had even predicted that every street in the city would be in good shape by February 4.

The politicians had helped diffuse tension by elevating unplowed streets to a status symbol. Wednesday morning, the *Courier-Express* published a front-page photograph of unplowed Roseville Street, where Mayor Makowski lived, and by midday politicians all over the city insisted that their streets remain unplowed, too. One councilman even removed the signs that had been posted to announce the plowing, and called the newspapers to demand that his street be removed from the plowing schedule.

"Every street posted was done," Lindner announced late Wednesday, "and that will continue to be the case unless we have another heavy snowfall."

About 460 cars had been ticketed, another 60 towed. And Lindner announced that the policy would get tougher—cars would be towed even from street' not especially posted for plowing if owners failed to respond to requests to move the vehicles. He told the public that he'd detail a plow to any street from which residents had managed to remove all cars, whether or not he'd scheduled it for plowing.

Foreman Danny Mango was talking to the skeleton crew when the commissioner entered the Broadway Garage at 5:30 that Thursday morning. "The big job right now," he was saying, "is to keep those main and secondary streets open. The 'blitz,' in case you didn't figure it out, is shelved."

He turned to the commissioner. "What're you doing here? Didn't I hear you on the horn one o'clock this morning?"

"*You're* here, aren't you?" said Lindner.

"Yeah, but I ain't the commissioner."

Lindner asked for an update on the equipment status. Thirty-three of the city's seventy-nine pieces of snow-removal machinery had broken down; much of it had been in use day and night since November, and that kind of punishment had to result in breakdowns—ruined engines, shot transmissions, even worn windshield wipers, all waiting for attention from the Motor Equipment Management Division, which repaired all the city's disabled vehicles in its own good time. At the moment, about half the division's men were off from work, five of them ill and the rest on vacation or personal leave.

Lindner himself was suffering personnel shortages. Of the seventy-two people on the snow-removal staff, seventeen called in sick Thursday morning. Of those who had reported, some had worked double shifts for months. A few had suffered heart attacks; one had suffered a nervous breakdown. Lindner had spent most of his time in the past month out on the road encouraging the men, assisting where he could, careful not to interfere when he couldn't contribute. It helped the men to know the boss was out there with them in the street. With nerves raw and bodies exhausted, those who could work continued to do so without complaint.

"I'm gonna see if the mayor'll get the governor to send help," Lindner told the crew. "The National Guard maybe, or the Department of Transportation. Otherwise—Christ, we're sitting ducks." He adddded a few words of encouragement, then left the garage.

A few minutes later, Lindner entered his office in the southwest wing of the fifth floor at City Hall. He greeted the secretaries and assistants briefly, offering encouragement with the grasp of a shoulder, a nod, a quick wave. This was no time for synthetically cheerful greetings—they'd all passed well beyond that. The secretaries had been taking hundreds of complaints a day, writing down each of them, patiently explaining why snow still hadn't been removed after weeks—in some cases, months—of promises. In response, they'd been screamed at, cursed, threatened. A week ago, one of the secretaries had run into Lindner's office crying. "It's the same every day," she wept. "I can't be here half an hour but I get a splitting headache. Why do they *curse* at me?"

One caller spoke to Lindner himself, warning him to get the roads open in three days or he and his family would be killed. Another threatened to bomb the Broadway Garage because a plow hadn't gone down his street all winter. A third man pulled a shotgun on a tow-truck driver for attempting to remove the gun-wielder's car from the middle of a street where it was blocking a plow.

In his office, Lindner turned on the police band. A car had broken down in the intersection of North Ogden and Williams streets, tying up traffic in four directions. Another vehicle was blocking a fire hydrant somewhere, and an ambulance driver complained that he couldn't get past abandoned vehicles to answer an emergency call.

Over the intercom, Lindner's secretary announced that a TV crew had come to interview him. He invited them into his office. The camera rolled, and a reporter demanded, "When are you going to whip your department into shape?"

*

That afternoon, the mayor said that New York's governor, Hugh Carey, had ordered the National Guard and Department of Transportation to help open Buffalo's streets. By evening, he promised, four heavy-duty snowblowers would go to work on Fuhrmann Boulevard and the Skyway. Ten snowplows would tackle the city streets, and two massive "wing" plows would clear the major arteries approaching and circling the city. Six National Guard high-lift loaders and a dozen trucks would remove the snowbanks encroaching upon the heavily traveled roads, and would dump the snow on the lake.

The mayor, in his City Hall office, seemed greatly pleased by the news. But Lindner received it over his car radio with pessimism. Certainly more equipment would help in clearing roads near hospitals and opening a few streets here and there. But lack of equipment was only one problem. There were two others that troubled Lindner even more.

The first was the sheer awesomeness of the weather. Literally millions of tons of snow lay upon the land. Winds of enormous force sprang into life to hurl it in blinding fury across hundreds of miles. Against such omnipotence the largest plow couldn't keep even a few blocks open. That afternoon Lindner himself had seen a street cleared practically to the pavement only to be closed by six-foot drifts forty-five minutes later. The awesome elements . . . the caprice of a jet stream, the momentary lingering of an air mass, and conceivably a hundred human lives could end in a mammoth Skyway snowdrift.

The second problem Lindner recognized was that the public would continue to frustrate clean-up efforts regardless of how much equipment was in use. Earlier in the day, Inspector John Reville had complained publicly that people "show absolutely no regard for their fellowman." Another officer had said, "They don't care, they just walk away and then they call up twelve hours later to find out where their car is." Sure, they're subject to fines, towing charges, even liability if someone, blinded by snow, runs into a car abandoned in a street. But what can the city do? Here it was, only midafternoon, and the police department had already received an estimated two hundred calls for a tow truck. The department itself had supplemented its fleet of two operating vehicles with another two from Dolan's Towing Company, but Dolan's had spent the morning towing fifteen cars off Fuhrmann Boulevard, and still hadn't reached the Skyway.

Even with the state's help, Lindner had his doubts. And, as though to confirm his fears, another squall hit the city with thirty-mile-per-hour winds at 1 P M The snow fell for two hours, then dispersed, with only an occasional flurry. Lindner admitted to a reporter who tracked him down at the Broadway Garage that the blitz to clear the city's side streets was off. Streets posted for plowing would not be reached until next week at the earliest. The best anyone could hope for was a holding action, keeping the main thoroughfares open.

*

In the midst of that afternoon squall, thirty-seven-year-old Jim Zinobile drove his sports car toward his home south of Buffalo. He didn't see the railroad tracks at Lake Avenue or the flatcar plow clearing them until he was upon them. In the collision, his face smashed into the windshield.

Earlier in the day, twenty-year-old Chris Ramsey approached another railroad crossing so cautiously that his car lost traction and stalled on the tracks. Through a fortunate break in the snowfall, Ramsey saw a train approaching and bailed out an instant before the car was demolished.

That afternoon, state and city plows cleared a path along Fuhrmann Boulevard to the Freezer Queen plant and liberated the more than two hundred workers who had been trapped there since Wednesday night. But plows failed to reach the Coast Guard base on the eddy jutting out into the lake where Fuhrmann Boulevard ended. Drifts reached fifteen feet there. The Coast Guard reported that, although the regular generator had failed, the emergency one had taken over. And food supplies were adequate for at least four days.

At the airport United, American, Eastern and Allegheny cancelled most flights because the sporadic squalls cut visibility to zero.

Buses out of the city ran generally on schedule, but some Amtrak trains were being delayed six to eight hours because near-zero temperatures and wind-driven snow from Chicago to New England had caused switching failures.

Buffalo State College's Department of Continuing Education cancelled its Thursday night lecture on survival techniques in cold weather.

The Erie County Parks Department announced a cancellation, too. The county's Fourth Annual Winter Carnival had already been rescheduled from January 23 to the coming weekend, January 29–30, because of too much snow earlier in the month. On Thursday, it was postponed again, this time until February 5–6. A few people appreciated the fact that the carnival's first two seasons had been handicapped by a complete absence of snow.

Late Thursday, Timothy Ryan, the American Automobile Association's Buffalo road service manager, told reporters that he'd received almost a thousand calls in twenty-four hours. Although the Automobile Club of Buffalo operates fifty-eight pieces of equipment, he said service had fallen a minimum of three hours behind.

On Thursday night, one of the winter's most serious crises came to a head in Albany. New York, along with several other northeastern states, had suffered severe heating-fuel shortages for more than a month, and on Thursday night Governor Carey finally declared a fuel emergency. The declaration set into motion plans to reallocate fuel supplies and restrict gas and oil use everywhere. Those violating the restrictions could be fined $1,000 per offense.

Almost simultaneously, the National Fuel Gas Company all but shut off natural gas to industries and drastically reduced the amount available to businesses, stores and schools. As a result, seven hundred and fifty industries in western New York, northwestern Pennsylvania and eastern Ohio announced Friday closings. Virtually all schools in the area did the same, and the stores and offices that remained open were ordered to set thermostats no higher than 55 degrees. Residents were requested to keep temperatures at 65 degrees or lower.

Girard C. Miller, general manager of National Fuel's Energy Services Division, told the press when he made the announcement, "We've been asking for voluntary cooperation for the last three or four days—and we got it this morning." But with the afternoon snowstorm and plummeting temperatures, the gas drain increased dramatically again and the company had to move quickly to conserve dangerously dwindling supplies.

"In a more normal winter, it would have taken until the end of February to use the amount of storage gas consumed so far this heating season," Miller said.

Thursday night the National Weather Service at the Buffalo International Airport predicted a cold Friday with lows near zero, along with the usual squalls and the now routine few more inches of snow, blowing into the routine drifts.

*

In spite of the mayor's assurances, neither the state's Department of Transportation nor the National Guard sent workers into the streets Thursday night, but representatives of both agencies did reach Commissioner Lindner and they planned a strategy meeting at Lindner's office in the Broadway Garage early Friday morning. The Department of Transportation would have available by then six pieces of equipment—primarily winged and V-plows. At the National Guard's Connecticut Street armory were thirty-six dump trucks, ten dozers and two graders. Four front-end loaders would be flown in from elsewhere in the state.

That night, Lindner was optimistic. He told reporters, "We're gonna get the best of this thing, guys. Give us a few days. Besides, we're looking for a reprieve from the weather. We need a break." He added somberly, "If we don't get one—God help us."

3

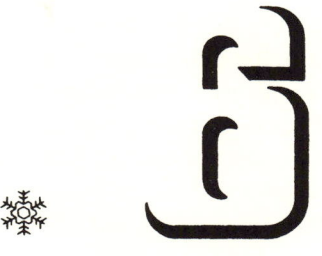

It probably happened something like this: When the long night came to the Arctic in November, a spray of ice crystals so fine as to appear a cloud of fluorescent dust in the moon's light soared upward in waves of rising air. Carried by erratic gusts, the cloud entered the upper limits of the troposphere, an altitude so great that the icebergs, far below, must have looked smaller than the tiniest snow crystals.

The capricious wind might have proved of little substance; it might have died, leaving the cloud to dissipate, the myriad crystals to glide through the rare atmosphere toward the earth. Some would have become embedded in the ice, while others dissolved in the vast ocean. A whale might have swallowed some and converted them to whale flesh, and a white bear might have done the same.

However, at least a handful of those crystals drifted into a secondary updraft. Hours later, the placid twilight suspension of ice dust was shattered in the rush of the west wind, the crystals battered against each other to an even finer powder and hurled southeast at staggering speeds.

Some fell into the Beaufort Sea, others into the uncharted regions of the Northwest Territories' Mackenzie Mountains. A few were swept eastward to Hudson Bay, to pass in decades hence through the Hudson Strait and into the Atlantic. The rest continued southward on the wind.

Moisture rising from the warmer earth over Alberta, Saskatchewan and Manitoba condensed on the ice, enlarging the crystals.

33

Some fell into Canada's forests and cities as a brief flurry, not raising an eyebrow. But the remaining crystals, although growing robust from the moisture they gathered to themselves, did not fall. Instead, closer to the heart of the wind, they continued southeast. Only in passing over Lake Superior did they finally drop to merge with the lake.

*

The water of Lake Superior flows southward into St. Marys River and the Sault Sainte Marie Canal. Great freighters burdened with ore and grain float upon it. Fishermen forage it and make bountiful catches. The water gathers in a great basin, Lake Huron, its sparsely populated banks to the north thick with oak and hickory forests, those to the south with birch, beech and hemlock. For a duration, the water might lay drifting without direction, warming and chilling, rising and falling in the same cycles as the atmosphere above, tugged by this current and that, and the passing ships and creatures of the lake.

The water of Lake Huron rushes under the International Bridge at Sarnia and Port Huron, flows into the St. Clair River, widens into a lake at St. Clair Flats. At Windmill Point it becomes the Detroit River, a twenty-eight-mile stretch with Detroit on one bank, Windsor on the other, a handful of islands in the river. Farther south, the banks widen, form the boundaries of another lake, more shallow than the rest, narrower except for one, its south shores teeming with cities and industry and summer homes. Lake Erie is the most violent of the Great Lakes, the most unpredictable and the most deadly. Some of the molecules of the Arctic's ice dust would find their way there.

Lake Erie: 240 miles long, 30 to 60 miles wide, stretching like a giant paramecium southwest to northeast across the map, from Toledo to Buffalo. Its mean depth reaches only 90 feet, and it is nowhere more than a shallow 210 feet.

As a river grows more tempestuous with the narrowing of its banks, so the wind, funneling into the closing eastern shores of the lake, stirs the water to increased frenzy. It spurts and boils as it never could in the deeper Huron. The wind drives the water eastward so that at Toledo, the depth drops by eight feet while, 200 miles away, it surges into the harbor at Buffalo. A shift in the wind's direction, and the rock bottom of the lake near Fort Erie is laid bare and the Ohio shore ravaged.

Subtropical highs from the south frequently stall over Lake Erie in their northern advance during the summer. And in the winter, the great bubble of polar air tumbles south to the same point. Not rarely, the warm and cold air collide over the lake causing wind storms explosive in their violence. One struck in November 1842, and dashed twenty huge ships against the north shore. Twenty-seven years later, another storm wrecked ninety-seven vessels, killing thousands of sailors.

The worst of all the Lake Erie storms occurred on Saturday, November 8, 1913. The weather bureau had predicted a falling of polar air from the north, wind from the west and southwest, and snow and rain. But no one had guessed that the wind would reach forty-eight miles per hour, or that the snow would be so heavy that navigation on the lake would be virtually impossible. The storm grew more furious Sunday and Monday, with winds of seventy-five miles per hour assaulting and crippling the lake cities—Detroit, Toledo, Cleveland and Buffalo—burying them under huge drifts. Telephone, telegraph and electric lines tore apart. Streetcars and trains stalled. A Cleveland conductor who went for help wandered blindly across the tracks and was run down by another train.

By the end of the week, more than a dozen ships and 2 barges had sunk, 26 vessels were swept ashore and destroyed or severely damaged, and 235 people had perished.

Exactly twenty-seven years later, on November 10, 1940, warm air from the south collided again with a polar front. The temperature fell from 63 to 25 degrees in four hours, then continued to drop to 15 degrees. Winds reaching 100 miles an hour pummeled Chicago, Detroit and Cleveland. They blew the shallow saucer of Lake Erie into awesome fury, draining the river ten feet below normal. Not as many ships sank as in 1913—they were better built in 1940. And fewer sailors drowned. But property damage was enormous, and at least one airplane crashed in the gale.

*

On December 14, 1976, the lake's temperature reached 32 degrees. Never since such records have been kept had the water grown so cold so early. By the end of the month, the lake had frozen over. In the air above it, the great forces, like disembodied gods, continued to war. One to the north, another to the south, the masses collided, feinted, retreated through two hundred miles of atmosphere, hurling each other toward earth or sky. Through all of January snow accumulated upon the ice. Some of it was fluffy, some composed of pure ice crystals, so fine it seemed upon falling a mere fog, a spray of dust. It never melted, but gathered in the eerie quiet.

On January 27 it covered the entire 10,000 square miles of the lake to a depth of three feet.

*

That day, while James Lindner pressed his department to open the streets and Bill Strobele dispatched police and fire equipment to rescue those newly stranded in Wednesday night's snow, radio and TV reporters half a continent away were warning the people of the northern plains to prepare for another Arctic cold front. Later in the day, the front tumbled with bitter fury across thousands of miles of open prairie, sweeping North Dakota and Iowa with snow and a windchill factor of 60 degrees below zero.

When the snow began falling in Iowa, Becky Tryon started home from work. The wind caught her car, hurling it off the road. She walked to the nearest farmhouse, but the people wouldn't let her in. The same thing happened at a second and a third home. As she stumbled along the road, a bus driver stopped for her and took her to a hospital. The doctors there diagnosed serious frostbite of the neck, ears and face.

The cold front surged across the Midwest from Minnesota to Illinois and south to Missouri. The windchill factor in Breckenridge, Minnesota, a small farming community, was minus 80 degrees, but a score of people found shelter in the old three-story Stratford Hotel there. That night a fire, whipped by savage wind, burned the wooden building to the ground, killing twenty-two people. Most of the bodies could not be removed, for they were buried in the ice when the million gallons of water pumped by fire engines froze.

The great high-wire walker Karl Wallenda lost control of his car on Ohio Highway Number Two near Mentor, skidded 180 degrees and stopped just short of plunging over the side of the highway. Police found him, helped him turn the car around and escorted him to the school where he was to perform. Wallenda told reporters there, "I've traveled all over the world in all kinds of weather, but I've never encountered anything to match that blizzard."

The Ohio roads, especially those in the southern part of the state, were particularly slippery because the salt needed by the state's Department of Transportation hadn't arrived—forty barges carrying 36,000 tons of it were trapped in the frozen Ohio River. So were another seventeen barges carrying salt needed in West Virginia.

There, especially in rural communities, the roads were impassable, and emergency food and fuel was being delivered by snowmobile.

The Mississippi River was frozen, too, making all navigation impossible for 160 miles north of Cairo, Illinois. With many highways also closed, transportation of essential food and fuel was coming to a standstill in the Midwest.

In Kentucky, the Army Corps of Engineers rescued 500 stalled barges of fuel oil, petroleum products and coal by raising the water level on sections of the Ohio River so that great chunks of ice blocking navigation dams might flow free. Then the barges broke their way through the ice upstream as far as Pittsburgh and Cincinnati.

The airports in Indianapolis and Cleveland closed. Amtrak cancelled twenty-eight trains in the midwestern, northwestern and northern plains because, as in Buffalo, the cold and snow had paralyzed switching yards and buried tracks beneath towering drifts.

Sports were cancelled everywhere. Racetracks closed in Chicago, West Virginia, Kentucky, Pennsylvania and Ontario, Canada. The NBA basketball game between the Buffalo Braves and the Cleveland Cavaliers was postponed because the Cavaliers couldn't leave their own airport. The Indiana-Iowa wrestling match was cancelled, along with the Northern Colorado and Western Illinois game. Promoters cancelled two U.S. Auto Club midget races, one in Indianapolis, the other in Louisville.

During the preceding week, the city of Erie, Pennsylvania, had averaged one burst water pipe an hour around the clock; the intense cold had penetrated three feet of earth, putting more than 750 pounds of external pressure on water pipes built to withstand less than half that. In a typical winter, the city could expect three or four frozen pipes per *year*.

*

Already the governors of Minnesota, Tennessee, Ohio, New York, Pennsylvania and New Jersey had declared energy emergencies, and some were talking of statewide disasters. In a dozen eastern and northeastern states, 8,900 industrial plants had closed and 548,000 workers were laid off because of the natural gas shortage. Governor James A. Rhodes of Ohio announced that there was "only enough gas available for the next several days to service residential customers, human needs and property protection." Suspending the Ohio Environmental Protection Agency regulations that prevent burning high sulfur coal, Rhodes urged industries equipped to do so to burn that fuel instead of natural gas. The state's gas-heated schools closed; the Reverend David W. Sorohan, superintendent of Roman Catholic Schools in the Columbus Diocese, said, "There isn't a prayer that any of us can stay open."

Schools were closed in several other states, too, among them Virginia, Pennsylvania, New York, New Jersey and Indiana. Governor Bowen of Indiana followed Rhodes's lead in suspending state and local pollution laws to permit burning of high-sulfur coal. The Northern Indiana Public Service Company ordered industries to cut back natural gas use to 10 percent of normal—just enough to prevent pipes from freezing.

In Georgia, several thousand families ran out of fuel and state officials worked desperately to get supplies re-allocated to those crisis areas.

Governor Milton Shapp of Pennsylvania asked President Jimmy Carter to declare a state of emergency there and to send extra natural-gas supplies. Appearing on the state's major television stations, Shapp appealed to all nonessential commercial enterprises to close at least until Monday to save fuel, and warned residents that they faced a serious threat of having no heat.

New Jersey's governor, Brendan Byrne, ordered almost all public buildings, apartment houses and hotels to turn down their thermostats to 65 degrees during the day, 50 at night. New York's Hugh Carey warned of widespread disruption unless the public heeded conservation warnings.

President Carter's chief energy advisor, James Schlesinger, told the House and Senate, while they weighed giving the President emergency authority to ration natural gas, "We are and have been using the gas that we expected to use in February and March. I think the full seriousness of the situation has not sunk in." Schlesinger suggested that if the President were not given power to re-allocate gas supplies, the residents of some hard-pressed areas would soon be without heat.

*

It was on September 26 of the previous year that Herbert Krone of Lancaster, Pennsylvania, had issued his forty-second annual Woolly Bear winter forecast. "This is the first time I've seen woolly bears with platinum-blond hair," he said. In fact, he hadn't seen such light hair on the creatures for more than half a century. It could have only one meaning, and Krone's prediction, carried by the Associated Press, appeared in 220 papers: "A very mild winter," he said. "I think there will be no winter at all!"

In fact, the prediction held true for the western third of the country, where the climate remained unseasonably warm and dry, with San Francisco reporting a drought crisis of unprecedented proportions. Restaurants served water only upon request. Officials estimated farm losses at one billion dollars. The legislators of exclusive Marin County, California, passed a water-rationing law tough enough to cut usage by more than 50 percent.

In south central Alaska, polar bears suffered in the stifling 40-degree temperatures and refused to hibernate.

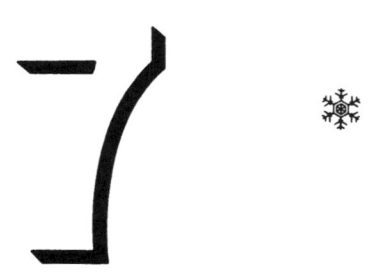

At 4 AM on Friday, January 28, 1977, Dick Rausch, night lead forecaster for the National Weather Service at Buffalo's International Airport, issued a "special" statement that had become routine during that severe winter. The travelers' advisory would be continued through the night, it said, for the seven western counties of New York:

> An intensifying low in Michigan this morning will move eastward, passing through western New York this afternoon. Snow will fall through much of today and tonight. As this developing storm center moves east of our area, very strong winds will once again produce near blizzard conditions beginning late this afternoon and continuing tonight. Accumulations of two to four inches are likely by evening, with more likely tonight.

Westerly gales behind the storm would cause drifting and poor visibility, and the accompanying Arctic air would bring wind-chill factors of 30 to 40 degrees below zero. People traveling late that afternoon and evening were warned to expect very difficult conditions.

The same forecast could have applied on a dozen days that winter: more snow, more drifts, more traffic jams, side roads uncleared for yet another week. Fortunately, it would be only a few inches, and wouldn't begin until late in the day.

That Friday, factories not affected by the gas cutoff along Fuhrmann Boulevard opened their doors again. Downtown department stores set thermostats low and prepared for a brisk business. Mayor Stanley Makowski took his fifteen-year-old son, Stanley, Jr., to church with him, then brought him to City Hall to observe firsthand the workings of government. The mayor called a meeting in his office to discuss the occupancy tax. The sun was shining.

About 210,000 vehicles converged upon Buffalo that Friday morning, most of them in single file, bumper to bumper along snow-clogged streets.

*

When Ben Kolker drove through a light snow into the airport parking lot, the weak sunlight did not deceive him. Now deputy meteorologist at the Buffalo office of the National Weather Service and two years from retirement, Kolker had spent every working day for thirty-eight years analyzing the weather. And one lesson he'd learned well was that, with the weather in Buffalo, nothing was necessarily as it appeared to be.

That morning Ben Kolker set a brisk pace from the parking lot to the airport. Hurrying up the escalator to the Weather Service office on the terminal's second floor, he nodded to the secretary and with somber face hurried through the front office. He'd already heard the earlier forecasts on the weather radio during breakfast, and two aspects of them aroused his concern: the conditions Rausch had forecast might require a blizzard warning, not the usual travelers' advisory. And that intensifying low-pressure area in Michigan was shaping up into a serious threat.

Dick Sheffield, the day-shift lead forecaster, who was getting ready to issue his late-morning forecasts, greeted Kolker as he walked into the forecast room: "Ben, I think we should issue a blizzard warning right away. Everything points that way."

Kolker turned to the charts and maps posted on the forecast room wall, noting the isobars, millobars, flags indicating wind speed and direction, temperature variations. He studied pressure gradients again more carefully. Then he skimmed the latest teletype reports from Toledo, Cleveland and Erie. All three cities were already reeling under a tremendous storm. Temperatures in Toledo had dropped 22 degrees in ninety minutes, from 20 degrees at 7 A M to 2 below at 8:30. The National Weather Service office in Erie had already warned all people in the vicinity to stay inside and said, "Travel might be disastrous." More than 500 accidents had already occurred in and around the city. Cleveland's Hopkins International Airport was closed, and office and factories were dismissing employees early.

"You're right, Dick," Kolker mumbled.

"Let's say the naughty word," said Sheffield. "We've got a real blizzard on our hands."

Standing nearby and listening to the conversation was Jim Smith, chief meteorologist in charge. Sheffield and Kolker both turned to him now. Smith nodded. "Go ahead," he said.

Until that moment, the National Weather Service at Buffalo had never described a winter storm as a blizzard. Although the National Weather Service considers a storm with winds of more than 32 miles an hour and visibility of less than 500 feet a blizzard, the winter storms of western New York differ in two important respects from the typical blizzard of the central plains: In Buffalo, the storms are "lake effect" squalls usually lasting no more than a few hours, and they are localized in the "snow belt"—south Buffalo and the counties immediately south and east.

In the past, the Buffalo Weather Service described severe snow storms as Dick Rausch had that morning—as "blizzardlike," or "near-blizzard conditions." To predict an actual blizzard, Kolker and Sheffield knew, would be to set a new policy, one that would lead to repercussions from superiors who didn't agree.

There was another effect a blizzard prediction might have, and it was far more serious than a skirmish with superiors. Such a forecast could lead to the closing of stores, offices and government agencies, and an economic loss to the area of several million dollars. Then— what if the blizzard never materialized?

But there was another question, and it held yet more serious implications: What if the blizzard did strike—and a couple of million people were caught without warning? Kolker hurried to his office to type the updated statement:

> Blizzard warning later this afternoon, and tonight. Winds becoming westerly, increasing to twenty to forty miles per hour with higher gusts at times during the afternoon and tonight—producing blizzard conditions in blowing and drifting. Occasional snow this afternoon accumulating up to three inches by evening. Bitterly cold with temperature five degrees above zero or colder by evening. Occasional snow likely tonight. Lows five to fifteen below zero, colder in some valleys.

By about 11 A M. the warning statement and forecasts had gone out on the statewide teletype circuits to all subscribers—newspapers, radio and TV stations, public utilities. And they were broadcast continually by tapes over the weather radio station in the office.

Ben Kolker glanced around the room. It was humming with activity—phones ringing, the nearest forecaster or radar specialist answering them, others checking and posting new charts and the latest teletype material, updating the radio tapes. Turning to the window, he could see across the roof of the airport terminal acres of snow-covered fields and runways, an airliner taxiing into position for takeoff. Visibility was a good three-quarters of a mile, cut somewhat by a few snowflakes drifting around in the light wind. The sun was dimly visible through the thin clouds. The thermometer outside the window registered a comparatively pleasant 26 degrees, and the wind was from the south. If it would only stay that way, they could maybe end up with balmy Caribbean breezes.

*

Elsewhere at the terminal, where the corridor leading to gates 10 through 15 ends, there are glass doors with black letters and an outer office with thick carpeting and green leather chairs. Behind that are inner offices. One of them is spacious, with windows overlooking the airport in three directions. It belongs to Richard F. Rebadow, general manager of the Greater Buffalo International Airport, and it was empty that Friday, for Rebadow was on his way to a funeral. His brother Robert, fifty-one, had died of a heart attack while shoveling snow in front of his home earlier in the week.

Next to the big office is a very small one, the walls of which were cluttered with newspaper clippings of Tammy Wynette, Neil Diamond, Emmy Lou Harris and the University of Miami football team. Three hanging plants overwhelmed the back of the room; almost directly beneath them sat assistant airport manager Bob Stone. He was thirty-four years old, had been at Buffalo International four years and was used to handling snowstorms. Ben Kolker had just phoned him, however, with the warning that this was no typical storm.

Still, he wasn't worried. Rebadow, his boss, had managed the airport for almost twenty-five years, and in that time he had forged an almost perfect machine. All airport supervisors and snow-removal personnel had long ago received bound copies of Rebadow's own "Snow Removal Operating Schedules, Regulations and Procedures," spelling out the overall approach to keeping the airport open. To mechanics and field personnel, Rebadow had issued a directive detailing required servicing procedures on an hours-in-operation basis for all snow-removal equipment. After twenty-four hours of use, plows would be checked top to bottom—shoes, bolts, arms, cables and frame—for stress breakage. Fluid lines, power steering, hydraulic brakes would be examined. Shear pins on the blowers would be checked, along with conveyor chains on the sanders. All vehicles would be started every four days and examined while running, and once every six months every piece of equipment would be exhaustively serviced. Every nut and bolt would be retightened, every gear and bearing lubricated.

The amount and caliber of the equipment was of the highest order. Although the airport had two runways, one of them was used 95 percent of the time, and to maintain it and the surrounding areas, the airport owned four runway brooms with a sixteen-foot capacity, three snow blowers, one of which had a 3,000-ton per hour capacity, six plows, two with thirty-foot capability, a snow dozer with a twenty-eight-foot blade, two trucks and three loaders.

Bob Stone wasn't worried about fighting a blizzard that morning—he'd simply put Richard Rebadow's perfect machine in action

*

While Ben Kolker had been studying the weather maps earlier that morning and Richard Rebadow was preparing to attend his brother's funeral, an attractive young woman was driving east on highway 130, a few miles south of the airport, toward the town of Depew. Rose Ann Wagner, a housewife and mother of two small children, spent Fridays waitressing at her mother's bar, Emil's Inn. Fridays were special at Emil's. The regular customers—local factory workers and truckers—came by to cash their paychecks and toast the end of another monotonous week, and the proprietress of Emil's Inn celebrated with a gala fish fry.

The drive to the bar was a quick one for Rose Ann, along the well-plowed four-lane highway known in Buffalo as Broadway. By 10:30 that morning she had almost finished setting tables.

"Radio says we're gonna have a blizzard," her mother, Irene, yelled from the kitchen.

"So what's new? Let it snow."

"And what am I supposed to do with a hundred pounds of fish when nobody shows up? You feel like eating a hundred pounds of fish?"

Rose Ann laughed. "They'll show up," she yelled. "They gotta cash their checks."

*

The instant the Oldsmobile's rear tires hit the dry concrete of the parking ramp, attorney Jeff Hensey floored the accelerator. The tires screeched and the car lurched ahead, the first time that morning it had moved more than a few miles an hour. He'd left his home in Hamburg an hour earlier than usual, aware that the Skyway where he'd been stranded for almost five hours Thursday morning was still closed. But the drive north along South Park was even more congested than he'd anticipated, and now, at almost 11 A M he was already ten minutes late for a hearing.

He wheeled the Oldsmobile into a "no-parking" area on the ramp and ran down toward the street, his tie and the tails of his unbuttoned overcoat flailing the air behind him.

He was almost to the courthouse before noticing the change in the weather. The wind had grown more brisk, and the sky was overcast.

*

In New York Telephone's executive offices on the sixteenth floor of the M & T Building in downtown Buffalo, Larry Mark, public relations supervisor of the company's western New York area, drew open the insulated drapes to reveal through floor-to-ceiling windows a panorama of the city, the frozen lake and the Pennsylvania and Canadian shores. Below him, across a complicated intersection, pedestrians on the parklike square before St. Paul's Cathedral ignored the light snow and waited for the street light to change.

Half-hidden behind the cathedral's gothic spires, on Franklin and Church Streets, the telephone company's nerve center, the central office building, raised its own steeple, a huge microwave tower. Two blocks farther west, the Buffalo Skyway arched against the background of the snow-covered lake.

Larry was addressing an informal strategy conference when, in the space of a few words, the sky grew dark—not merely the graying of an overcast day or the bleakness of a rainy afternoon, nor the absolute blackness of night, but the peculiar shadowless gray-brown gloom of an eclipse.

Beyond the Skyway, the world had vanished—Canada, the Pennsylvania shore, the rugged hills. All had merged into the dark gray sky, streaked as though someone were erasing a charcoal sketch section by section, leaving the paper an opaque smudge.

The room grew silent. Everyone turned to the windows. They heard a roar an instant before the wind struck the building. Larry felt the floor shudder and heard the plate glass creak.

Sixteen floors below, shoppers and businessmen staggered into the wind. Some clung to street-light poles and traffic signs; others ducked for shelter. A man's hat soared high above traffic.

"Holy Christ," the division manager muttered.

He joined Larry at the window to watch the colossal wave of gray roll ominously over the shore.

In that instant the Skyway disappeared. A few seconds later, the Ellicott Square building was blotted out, along with the cars, people and lights below.

New York Telephone's central office vanished simultaneously with its microwave tower, then the church steeple across the street ceased to exist.

The instant the white wave struck the window, Larry wondered if the world might be ending.

The time was 11:10.

*

Ed Janak was the tall, lean, unassuming assistant regional highway maintenance engineer for the state's Department of Transportation. He was responsible for keeping state highways and bridges in four western New York counties open and in good repair, and although emergencies had occurred on occasion—usually bridge washouts—the job was usually routine and predictable.

Along with his primary title, Ed Janak had been given a second one the year before. When a severe ice storm during the winter of 1976 had made roads murderously slick, Janak coordinated salting and other efforts and got them open promptly. Thus, his boss, David Piper, dubbed him Regional Disaster Coordinator. Ed joked at the time that the title's main significance was that now everyone knew he would get stuck working overtime for the next ice storm.

But it came as a surprise on Thursday when Dave Piper told Janak that he had been called to coordinate the state's efforts in unclogging Buffalo's streets.

"It's your job," Piper had told him Thursday. "You've got DOT's equipment and you've got the National Guard."

Driving to a 9 A.M. meeting with Lindner and Guard liaison officers Friday morning, Janak found particular humor in his boss's words. In the army, Janak had made specialist first class. Yet, the weather and circumstances had promoted him to commander of all the National Guard troops who would be assisting in the snow removal—even regular army soldiers, perhaps. Janak had no idea what to expect.

He did not anticipate, for example, the horde of media representatives that greeted him at the Buffalo garage that morning. The weather—gas shortages, frozen citrus crops and Buffalo's battle with the snow—had been the lead story all week long on network newscasts; photos of Buffalo's streets adorned the front pages of the nation's newspapers. Now, with the news that the National Guard was coming to the city's rescue, TV cameramen, photographers, Associated Press and United Press International reporters and sound technicians joined writers from the local newspapers in converging upon the Broadway garage. It was, thought Janak, a bit much.

Also at the meeting were Lieutenant Colonel Gerald Harris of the National Guard, Lindner and Lindner's deputy, James Pierakos, and several assistants; after various interviews and photographs the men sat down to plan a strategy. Lindner issued pocket radios to everyone so that they could keep in touch at all times; Janak was issued the handle NY-1; his assistant, NY-2; Harris, G-1; Lindner, U-1; Pierakos, U-2. Lindner would issue a plan of operation listing the city's streets according to priority and tell Janak which jobs the city's own crews would be handling. Janak would assign the rest to Harris and the DOT crews and keep tabs on the work completed and still to be done.

It would take time to get the wheels in motion. The plan still had to be drawn—that could be done in a few hours. But the National Guard had yet to be mobilized, cold-weather gear flown in along with heavy snow-removal equipment. Even some of the DOT equipment and crews had not yet reached the city. Janak decided to put DOT equipment to work as it arrived, and city crews were already out on the streets, but the National Guard would not begin until Monday night at 8 P M, after rush-hour traffic had dispersed, and they would work a twelve-hour shift.

At 11:30 that morning, as the meeting was about to adjourn, one of Lindner's plows rumbled into the garage. A moment later it was followed by another, then another. A driver came into the meeting, his face reddened by the wind.

"It's snowing like hell out," he told Lindner. "Christ, we can't do a thing—can't even see the plow blades!"

A moment later, another came to announce, "We lost Main Street. We just can't *see* "

Lindner's face grew red, but he said nothing.

Finally, as the men were preparing to leave, another crewman straggled in. Lindner stopped.

"What the hell are you doing here?" Lindner demanded. "You're supposed to be down by City Hall. Who's keeping the square open?"

"Look, boss," the man said, then paused. He dropped his head. "We lost the square."

"We *can't* lose the square!" Lindner bellowed. "That's it—that's the city! We never lose the square!"

3

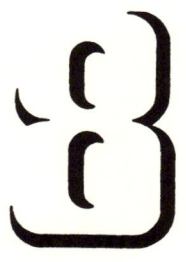

Bill Strobele, the Buffalo police dispatcher, left the supermarket at Abbott Road Plaza with arms full of groceries. He stopped abruptly. Ten minutes earlier, when he'd driven into the parking lot, the sun had been shining. Now his car and the entire parking lot had vanished in a fury of snow. Strobele had lived in Buffalo all his life—forty years—and had never seen so violent a snowfall, tiny crystals as dense and impenetrable of vision as any dust storm.

There was no alternative to waiting for the nuisance lake squall to subside. Following the wall of the building, he found his way to Kresge's, a restaurant not far from the supermarket, and took a seat near the window.

"Damnedest thing I ever saw," the waitress said. "Radio says it's gonna be a blizzard."

Forty-five minutes later, Bill Strobele still sat at the window, sipping coffee and watching with fascination the snow's unrelenting accumulation.

*

When the storm hit the Salvation Army Headquarters on North Main Street, a few blocks from the *Courier-Express* office, the building was almost deserted. An hour earlier, about two hundred elderly members of the Golden Age Club had been involved in the day's program, but when Major Bob Williams heard the weather forecast, he decided to send everyone home immediately. And Captain Geoffrey Banfield, realizing that travel would be much more difficult later in the day, told the staff to take the afternoon off. Thus, when the snow came, Williams and Banfield and a handful of procrastinating Golden Age Club members were the only ones remaining in the building.

*

During the hearing on the occupancy tax in his outer office, Mayor Stanley Makowski felt the change in temperature. A cold breeze fluttered the papers on his desk, and his first thought was that someone had opened a window. He turned to the window facing the lake and was momentarily puzzled by the eerie darkness. Moments later he saw nothing but the crushing whiteness.

He turned to those in the room for advice and finally determined to make an announcement. With his son at his side, he prepared a statement allowing department heads to decide whether or not to dismiss their staff early. Then he called deputy mayor Les Foschio and asked him to take charge.

*

By 11:30 most of the city's businesses and industries were releasing workers early. People by the thousands rushed into the downtown streets, to be startled by the storm's fury. Those who stepped away from the buildings staggered under the wind's assault. A few fell into snowbanks, others walked into parked cars.

Trusting to memory and aided by the occasional moments when the onslaught abated and the air grew still, some found their way to parking lots and their automobiles. Only a few reached home. The remainder struggled futilely to start their cars, or starting them, became entangled in crippling traffic tie-ups long before reaching the city's outskirts. Thousands of them abandoned their cars in roadways and continued on foot, seeking shelter in police stations, firehouses, bars—anywhere they were welcomed.

Others hurried to bus stops, clung to poles or the sides of buildings to await the buses, but could not endure for more than a few minutes. Dazed, they wandered into stores and hallways to grow warm again. Dozens developed frostbite.

Many didn't even step outside the buildings, but stared dumbly through glass doors, pondering the alternatives, awaiting a slackening of the wind. Thousands turned back to their offices to wait out the squall. At City Hall, hundreds returned to their desks.

Still others found their way to coffee shops, bars and cocktail lounges. Attorney Jeff Hensey was among them. He'd left the courthouse as angry as he had entered it twenty minutes earlier—the judge had not appeared for the hearing, but had telephoned the secretary and dictated a note that a blizzard would strike the city and everyone should go home.

But Jeff Hensey took only a few steps in the snow before turning back to the courthouse to shake off his collar, turn it up and button it tightly around his neck. He pulled the leather gloves from his pocket. What a damned, miserable, hopeless winter, he thought. Well, there'd be no repeat of Wednesday night. Then he'd been stranded on the Skyway more than four hours—and only a hundred feet from an exit. He'd devoted the day Thursday to finding a tow company capable of winching the car from the ramp to Tifft Street, and when it was done, it cost him $69.37 and a twisted bumper. But at least he had the Oldsmobile. Now he'd get to the car and he'd get home, the blizzard be damned.

Hensey had a solid, muscular body, weighed 182 pounds and was almost six feet tall, but he still found it an effort to maintain his balance against the wind. Striking his back, it pushed him into a jog.

The snowbanks warned him of the intersections, for he could see neither traffic lights nor autos until he came upon them. But soon he lost the fear of being crushed beneath the tires of a car bursting suddenly out of the whiteness for, with zero visibility, few people were driving. Many had abandoned their cars in the streets, a few in the intersections. Snow had already accumulated around them, reaching the axles and bumpers. An occasional bus lumbered by at not more than a mile or two an hour, its grinding engine giving ample warning of its approach. Passengers crushed themselves into every available space within it, steaming the windows with the moisture of their breath.

At the intersection of Franklin and Niagara, Jeff hesitated. To the left was the parking deck and the Oldsmobile, but now driving seemed out of the question. He could go to the car and wait, or he could find some other place to wait out the squall. Directly ahead on Niagara was Main Place Mall, and he decided to wait there.

Hundreds of people were congregated at the doors there, staring blankly into the whiteness. Jeff shouldered his way through the crowd to the center of the mall, where he found some breathing space. He'd walked no more than a block but already his gloved fingers ached with the cold and his face had become numb.

Fifteen minutes later, with the storm still raging, Jeff decided to have lunch. He spent an hour in the restaurant, another thirty minutes pacing the two floors of the mall, now more crowded than ever. It occurred to him that the storm could go on for hours. He would not spend the time pacing the mall, he decided. He'd try to get to McTrevor's.

McTrevor's was a corner bar which, for no other reason than its strategic location, had become a gathering place for the white-collar sorts who shunned the sophisticated lounges. After a particularly tough trial, Jeff and a few colleagues often gathered there to either congratulate or console one another, often buying drinks for the local boozers who spent the better part of every day there.

Pushing through the crowd again, Jeff stepped out onto Main Street. It seemed the wind had grown even stronger, and now Jeff had to walk at an angle to it, across the great open intersection at St. Paul's Cathedral. So dense was the snow that he could see neither the cathedral to his right nor the towering M & T Building. Walking along the center of the street, he crossed Main, then Washington, proceeded south for a block almost directly in the face of the wind, and at the corner of Washington and Swann stumbled into McTrevor's.

A cheer greeted him as he stepped inside. "Another sheep returns to the cesspool," someone yelled.

"Bet your face stings," said a tall, pretty girl. Her brown, shoulder-length hair was tangled around her neck and she was trying to straighten it with her fingers.

"Burns like hell—my feet ache, too."

"Tell me about it," she said knowingly. She brushed the snow from his hat and shoulders.

"Buy you a drink?" he asked.

*

The phone at the National Weather Service offices rang without cease. At twenty-two minutes after eleven the sky over the airport, eight miles northeast of downtown Buffalo, had taken on a peculiar darkness, although only light snow had yet fallen. But half a dozen callers had already made it clear that the center city area was at that moment seized by yet another storm.

"You're a bunch of *jackasses*, that's all," a husky voice shouted into the ear of Ed Reich, assistant forecaster. "Why the hell didn't you *say* it was coming this *morning*, instead of this *afternoon*? You shoulda *known* something like that—that's what you get *paid* for!"

"You *demand* to know when it's going to stop?" an incredulous meteorologist asked another caller. "I'd like to know myself, now that you mention it. Yeah, well, we're confused, too. Two, three hours maybe—that's a guess, but there's just not enough moisture in the air for it to go on snowing all day."

On the other side of the forecast room, sitting alone, Ben Kolker studied the data sheets again. His face was somber, and he was so absorbed that he heard neither the jangling phones nor the unusually animated dialogue among the staff.

Finally, he pushed back his chair, clasped his hands behind his head and stared out the window. It's that damned low over Michigan, he thought. Only, it's not over Michigan any more. It's somewhere northeast of us, up in New England and Canada, and it's sucking that heavy, cold air toward it like a colossal vacuum pump. It's pulling the cold front halfway across the country, clear across the lake, unusually high speeds. That's why it got here so quick.

Still, there was some cause for optimism. Already some of the weather stations west of Lake Erie were reporting that, after a few hours, the snow was tapering off. It would be an intense storm, certainly—but, one could hope, brief.

Ben watched an Eastern Airlines plane taxi into position for takeoff to warmer Miami. Then he saw, behind it to the west, a white wall. It approached at incredible speed, sweeping everything in its path into oblivion. The windows of the Weather Service office trembled and the cold wind rushed through the cracks causing a perceptible drop in temperature in the forecast room.

In a moment, the wall of snow rushed upon the airliner, engulfed it, moved toward the terminal, causing ground service vehicles and the pavement to vanish. When it struck, the building shuddered. A loose window flew open and the blast sent maps and charts flying. In seconds the window became as frosted glass.

*

While the Eastern Airlines flight to Miami idled on the runway awaiting clearance for takeoff, two more planes taxied into position close behind it. Now all three were stranded in zero visibility and ceiling. Checking with Ben Kolker at the Weather Service, control tower personnel learned that the storm wouldn't break for hours, and called the planes back to the gate, beginning with the Eastern flight. But in the five minutes the jet had idled in the storm, its nose wheel had frozen, and the pilot couldn't steer to turn the plane around. The Eastern flight blocked those behind it from turning, so all three planes and hundreds of passengers remained on the runway.

Nearby, several plows had lined up like a row of tanks to do battle the moment the blizzard struck, but when the impenetrable snow drove into them, spraying through the loose-fitting doors and windows of the cabs, the foreman told the other drivers to leave the vehicles idling and come immediately to his plow truck. With five shivering drivers cramped into the cab, the truck crawled back toward the garage.

Another maintenance man was driving a small pickup truck off the terminal ramp when a gust blasted snow through the grill, around the radiator and onto the engine block. The snow melted, saturating the spark plugs and stalling the engine. After a few minutes, he left the vehicle and started toward the garage.

He couldn't see beyond a few yards, however, and soon lost his sense of direction. Above the wind's howling, he heard the roar of jet engines and the faint rumble of trucks. He turned from the sounds, certain the garage would not be in those directions, and headed blindly across the field.

From a temperature of 26 degrees earlier in the day, the thermometer had already plunged to zero, and now, with gusts reaching fifty miles an hour, the man's body quickly grew numb. He wandered in circles until, fearful he wouldn't survive more than a few more minutes, he started toward the sound of the trucks. About to collapse from exhaustion, he stumbled into one of the plows left idling on the field.

Even in the cab, with the heater operating at maximum, he felt the profound cold. He lifted the microphone and called for help. The tower answered, and half an hour later he was back at the terminal being treated for frostbite.

Scrutinizing the now opaque windows of his office unceasingly, Assistant Manager Bob Stone spoke by phone with maintenance supervisors all over the airport. It seemed impossible, yet the story was the same in every corner: The perfect machine had failed. Snow was accumulating on the runways every minute, and the fact that pilots couldn't see to take off or land was academic—flights were impossible because Buffalo International Aiport was in fact closed to traffic.

9

The drive from Abbott Road Plaza to Bill Strobele's home is about four blocks, but at 1 PM, the police dispatcher had been behind the wheel for almost an hour. During the frequent periods of zero visibility, Bill brought the car to a stop and waited. When he could see ten or twelve feet again, he moved at a crawl, scouring the road for stalled cars, snow drifts, pedestrians. Often, after a fierce whiteout abated, the car would be bogged down. Finally rocking it free, he'd be barraged again by blinding snow.

At Densmore he turned left from Onondaga. For another ten minutes the car inched through bumper-high snow. Bill stopped beside a telephone pole, the first landmark he'd recognized—he'd driven several houses too far. Backing up was out of the question: Half a foot of snow already buried the rear window, and even if he brushed it off, it would accumulate again before he could get back in the car.

He drove into a nearby driveway with torturous concentration, spent another ten minutes turning the car around and heading back the way he'd come. Futilely he searched for the chain-link fence surrounding his house. Finally, putting the car in park, he climbed the snowbank and searched for the fence. He was almost upon it when he saw the snow-covered links. He'd stopped the car practically in front of the house.

Mary Strobele met her husband at the door, her concern still obvious in her face. Bill told her of the difficult drive, and said he'd have to leave for work immediately.

55

"Think you can make it?"

He shrugged. "Yeah, I think so—not with the car. I'll take the bus."

"I'll pack you a big lunch."

A few minutes after two, he left the house wearing two pairs of pants and socks, a police shirt, sweater, insulated vest, cap with earflaps, hooded jacket, gloves, boots and scarf. During the half hour he'd been inside, another foot of snow had accumulated, making the short walk along Densmore to Abbott Road and the bus stop an exhausting effort. He noticed not a single pedestrian along the way, and the street seemed desolate and silent but for the occasional whistle of wind and the whooshing of snow crystals against his hood.

Upon reaching the bus stop, he found no traffic on the usually busy Abbott Road. After several minutes a single car drove past, slowly, its sounds muffled.

Wrapping the scarf around his face and tucking it into his hood, Strobele resigned himself to a long wait. Twenty minutes passed with only a handful of cars creeping by and no buses. They might be snowbound, he thought. Still, he endured, hopping from foot to foot, clapping his hands to fight the cold now beginning to penetrate the layers of socks and shirts and trousers. Finally he trudged to the dry cleaner on the corner and asked to use the phone.

His fingers were too rigid and painful to turn the dial, and minutes later, when they began to grow warm, they felt as though they'd been impaled by glowing hot needles. Dialing was torment, but he finally reached Metro.

"How should I know if they're running?" an information staff member demanded. "I'm not out there, I'm in *here*."

"Well, this is Officer Strobele, and I've got to get to Police Headquarters."

"Oh. Well, if you put it that way—we got some buses out, but I ain't gonna promise you'll get one. They're stuck all over the place. You got another way downtown, you take it now before the snow piles up real bad. Sorry I can't tell you nothing else—I ain't out there, you know—I'm in *here*."

Strobele dialed another number. Lieutenant John Flicinski answered at police headquarters.

"I don't know how I'm gonna get in," Strobele told him.

"That's great. That's just great—how the hell am I supposed to run a department? *Nobody's* coming in!"

"Well, I'm on Densmore and Abbott. You send me a bus and I'll come in—or send a helicopter for all I care."

Lieutenant Flicinski was quiet for a moment. Then he said, "Listen, go across the street—see the Exxon station? My son's there—drives a tow truck. Tell him I said he should run you in if he gets the chance. His name's Mike."

Mike was about to leave to jump start a car with a dead battery, and he invited Bill along for the ride. They headed northwest on Abbott, then turned left into Woodside. Mike stopped the truck.

"See? They do it every time," he bellowed. "Call for help, then get the damned car started and don't even give us a lousy call. It makes me so freaking mad!" He slammed the truck in reverse. "I'll take you to work," he told Bill. "I dig driving in this stuff anyways, 'specially when I can't see where I'm goin'!"

The truck lunged ahead, the youth maneuvering steadily around the stalled and stranded cars that appeared with fearful suddenness.

At the junction of Abbott and South Park, Mike repeatedly sounded the horn, crossed the intersection and continued downtown on South Park. For a quarter of a mile, this more direct route seemed the wise choice. Then, at Hopkins Street, a block before the upgrade to the railroad crossing, they came upon a tangle of cars. Mike jumped out, jogged past the first few and vanished. Soon he reappeared.

"Christ, they're all over the place, every which way, all the way to the tracks. Looks like it's the same story on the other side—a little hill, they go too damn slow, lose traction, and that's the end of that story. Well, I ain't licked yet."

Mike threw the truck in reverse, climbed over a snowbank lining the sidewalk, slammed the shift into forward and drove back to Abbott Road. There he made a sharp left on Bailey and headed north toward Seneca Street, which parallels South Park. Both end at Main Street in downtown Buffalo.

For a while the snow seemed to fall less heavily, and Mike weaved between the stalled cars at a steady fifteen miles an hour. He crossed Milton and Imson and Wasson streets, impassable alleys now with snow deep enough to bury cars. Northwest of Wasson was a railroad crossing, but the few cars stalled near it offered no difficulty for Mike, who maintained a steady speed up the incline. But beyond that, at Fillmore, was another crossing, and there Mike and Bill saw a tie-up that made the one at Hopkins look minuscule by comparison.

Apparently a driver had slowed to a crawl in approaching the tracks, and with no momentum had lost traction on the incline and skidded perpendicular to the road. The car behind him avoided a collision by driving off the right shoulder, while a third car had driven off the left.

A similar story had unfolded on the west side of the tracks, and cars, some with headlights gleaming through the snow, extended into a white infinity.

"It goes like that for about three blocks," Mike exclaimed upon returning from a brief investigation. "No problem—I'll go back to Babcock, up to Clinton Street, over to William—."

"No, it's gonna be the same all over the place," said Bill. "Besides they're gonna need you back at the garage. I'll walk."

"You're crazy, man! That's gotta be three or four miles yet, and the wind's blowing like hell. You're gonna wake up dead in some snowbank."

Strobele laughed. "If I get cold, I'll knock on somebody's door. Look, thanks a lot—you made it a lot easier."

"Yeah, sure. Maybe I signed your death warrant. Well, good luck."

Bill Strobele stepped out and slammed the door. The first blast of wind-driven ice tore savagely at his face. He'd expected it, and yet it caught him unprepared, staggering him, taking his breath. Leaning into the wind, he started toward the lake.

At the crossing, he wound between the cars, climbing the drifts that had formed between them, a maze of such complexity that it seemed only a brilliant mind could have engineered it. Stumbling over a bumper, sliding across a hood, he moved through the confusion for several blocks, until the massive tie-up dwindled to a semi-orderly line, bumper to bumper, all with headlights and engines off. As he passed each car, he brushed the snow from a window and looked inside. They were all abandoned.

God help the poor fool who's waiting for *this* line to get moving, he thought.

He was approaching the end of the line, but then more cars appeared, falling into formation, the drivers turning off headlights and engine, leaving their vehicles and moving like lemmings across a parking lot and into a bowling alley. Farther along, fifteen or twenty hurried toward a tavern. Others sought shelter in a corner store.

He'd walked only about three long blocks, but he knew he'd soon have to seek shelter himself. His face felt as though it were in a plaster cast—even his eyelids moved stiffly. Ahead, at the fork where Seneca veered left and Swann Street right he saw Engine 32, the Seneca Street Firehouse. He'd stop there to knock off some snow and ice and warm up a little, perhaps beg a cup of coffee. Then he just might be able to make it all the way to headquarters.

Other silent, snow-muted forms moved like shadows toward the building. They approached by the dozens from every direction across the land, along both Seneca and Swann and from the nearby factories.

A few firemen, recognizing the police uniform, took him to a seat in their private quarters and gave him a cup of coffee. They talked with enthusiasm about the storm, and Bill told them all he'd seen.

"It's gonna go on like this all night—that's what the weatherman says, anyhow," said one of the firemen. "First it's gonna stop, then it's gonna go. I wish the damn weatherman would make up his mind."

"Pray God we don't have a fire is all I can say," another commented.

Fifteen minutes after he entered, Bill put on his coat and two hats, gloves and scarf, and left the firehouse. It was 3:30 then.

*

In the large, dark room next to the forecast room, Ben Kolker and the radar specialist studied the radarscope again. Neither the storm's fury nor the snow's density had abated in almost four hours, yet it seemed impossible that it could continue much longer.

For one thing, stations west of Buffalo had sent teletype reports that the storm had lasted only a couple of hours and there seemed no reason to doubt the same would be true of Buffalo. More importantly, by 1:30 that afternoon, the radarscope, with a range of 250 miles, had shown virtually no snow in the upper air. On that basis, the Weather Service had predicted that the storm would stop. Now, it was obvious they had made a mistake.

The snow was coming not from the clouds but from the lake, the 10,000 square miles of it, and the vast open land surrounding it. Several rare circumstances had occurred simultaneously: a record-breaking accumulation of snow; temperatures so cold that the lake had frozen very early in the season, allowing the snow to build up there; continuing cold temperatures so that, unlike most years, the snow did not melt and pack tightly but remained as it had fallen, in fine, loose crystals; a deep low-pressure area had helped to create violent winds that swept the snow before them.

No more than two to four inches of fresh snow would fall in the next twenty-four hours but it was anyone's guess how much blowing snow would cover Buffalo. It would go on accumulating until the wind abated or shifted, or until the snow crystals, driven at great speeds, packed and fused solidly.

It was this revised forecast—blizzard conditions continuing indefinitely into the night—that the city's citizens heard late that afternoon.

*

Bill Strobele continued west on Seneca Street through a commercial and industrial neighborhood, with railroad tracks and factories that stretched south even beyond South Park. It was a desolate, open terrain now, across which the wind roared with particular fury from the lake a few miles southwest, its path virtually unimpeded. The snow accumulated rapidly against the cars, but did not gather on the windward side, for it was swept from there by the unceasing wind. Instead, the dry, dustlike crystals fell into the relatively placid eddies behind the cars, and it was there, on the downward side, that the snow now rose to the door handles.

Yet in an instant, with a shift in the wind's direction, the entire drift pattern would change. A screaming gust would lift an incalculable tonnage of snow, fine and cold and unpacked, and hurl it for blocks. It was under such an onslaught that Bill Strobele progressed.

Against certain buildings, particularly those with L-shaped corners, the wind did not sweep the snow clear but drove it into drifts already fifteen feet high. So forcefully were the crystals driven that they shattered and fused into each other, forming hills of ice that would support Strobele's weight without yielding so much as a footprint.

After traveling only two blocks from the fire station, the endlessly long ones of industrial neighborhoods, Bill's face grew numb again and his feet ached with cold. He decided to stop at the Seneca Street Police Garage, where the department's vehicles were serviced and repaired. It was another two blocks away, at Seneca and Louisiana, and he increased his pace against the wind.

He tried to imagine what he would look like to another traveler on this stretch of now-abandoned road, leaning forward at such a radical angle that, should the blowing stop for an instant, he would certainly fall flat on his face. Something of an abominable snowman, no doubt.

Approaching Louisiana, he noticed some activity. Three cars were blocking the intersection, the snow already over their bumpers, and a police officer on a three-wheel motorcycle was gesturing frantically to one of the motorists to move his car and clear at least part of the street for passing traffic. But the car lacked sufficient traction to plow through the snow. The officer left the motorcycle and pushed the car, and it began moving. At that moment, a two and a half ton truck approached the intersection, drove into a snowbank and stalled, blocking the other vehicles.

The police officer threw up his hands in disgust.

"Forget it," he yelled at the people in the cars. "You better get out and find someplace warm." He started his three-wheel motorcycle, zoomed around the cars and into the driveway of the Seneca Street Garage. Bill started after him, then decided instead to walk another block, to Chef's Restaurant. It was owned by his old friend Lou Billittier and he knew that, if nothing else, he could at least count on a cup of strong coffee.

It was 4:30 and almost dark when he entered Chef's.

People had crowded into each of the restaurant's several spacious dining rooms and stood in lines from the phone booths that extended across the restaurant. Lou Billittier himself sat near the door.

"How about a cup of coffee for somebody that's freezing half to death," said Bill. The restaurant owner surveyed him casually. "If you'd introduce yourself, maybe I could spare a cup of coffee for a new friend," he said.

"*New* friend? You trying to tell me you don't know who I am just to save a cup of coffee?"

"How the hell should I know who you are? You got snow all over you. I can't even see your face. So who the hell are you?"

Strobele turned to the mirror on the wall. His reflection startled him—snow clinging to his face, icicles literally hanging from his eyebrows, the moisture of his breath caked as frost above his upper lip. Although he hadn't realized it, his eyelids had frozen into a squint. Not only the snow, but his face seemed to melt as he watched, and the swelling pain resembled fire more than ice. He started to laugh, but it was too painful.

Strobele formally introduced himself, and Lou Billittier, always cool, always suave, gaped in astonishment. He sent a waitress for the coffee, led Bill to a seat at his private table and called a doctor from an adjoining room.

10

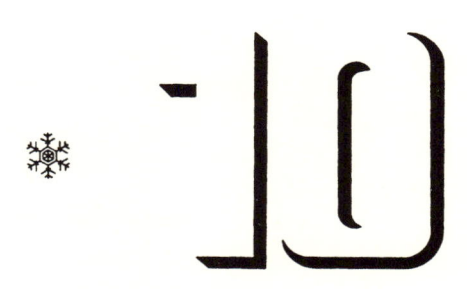

Sixty-three-year-old Joe Falzone placed the last of the numerous locks on the door of his delicatessen. The Falzone store and home two doors away were on Virginia Street and Whitney Place, several blocks north of City Hall and a few blocks east of the lake, and since 11:30 that morning, the barrage of snow had overwhelmed the neighborhood. The typical flow of customers had dwindled until, during the past hour, none at all had walked through the doors. Joe Falzone had started that store in 1932 and, although the neighborhood had changed since then, with an upsurge in minorities and low-income families, the people had always been steady customers and good friends; there never had been five minutes without a customer, much less an hour. Not until today. Joe decided to close early.

With the store securely bolted, he walked along Whitney Place to his home. People were gathered in the street trying to push a car out of the single lane that was still open. Another vehicle was stuck in the intersection, but had been moved sufficiently to allow cars to pass. The snow was rapidly accumulating, almost up to Joe's knees now, and soon it would be impossible for any but four-wheel drives to get through.

In the snow, the neighborhood's blight was imperceptible, and for a moment Joe Falzone reflected upon the years past. Even the house next to the store, the white clapboards faded, the wooden frame decaying, seemed more stately behind the veil of snow, the windows glowing with the diffused lights and black smoke billowing from the chimney. In fact, on all the block, Falzone knew his was the only newly remodeled house. Through all the years he had kept it in superb condition, not only through personal pride but also to challenge the other property owners to do the same. Yet, every year the city condemned more houses in the neighborhood, and more people, fearing the high crime rates, sold and moved to the suburbs.

Still, it was home, this house on Whitney Place. Joe's wife had moved into it when she was a year old, fifty-nine years ago. Their children had been born and raised there, and someday it would be young Joe Paul's. Through the years they'd remodeled it and decorated it and furnished it, until now it was just the way they wanted it. And maybe the neighborhood was improving, too. There were fewer transients, and a nearby bar, known for its violence, had closed.

Joe heard a familiar voice call his name. His son, Joe Paul, waved from the corner and ran to unlock the house door for him. They climbed the stairs together, talking about the incredible snow.

*

In the kitchen at Emil's Inn, Rose Ann Wagner caught the WKBW weather forecast:

> Blizzard conditions tonight with extremely strong winds gusting over fifty miles an hour will cause serious blowing and drifting of snow as temperatures drop to minus ten by morning. The windchill reading will reach sixty below zero. Tomorrow, continued very windy and extremely cold with snow flurries, snow squalls, blowing and drifting. There'll be little change on Sunday. Temperatures tomorrow will be mainly below zero. The high Sunday—plus five degrees.

Bursting into the bar with still more plates of fried fish, Rose Ann cheerfully repeated to a gang of celebrating customers the latest weather forecast. It was received jovially, and someone even proposed a toast to the blizzard. Most of the men had come to cash their pay checks at noon, and while others had left immediately, this group of eighteen had decided to wait out the squall. Now they had no hope of leaving.

The spirit was festive, boisterous, with good-natured jokes about who would spend the night with Rose and her mother. The women offered everyone free coffee.

At about 5 P M , sixty-four-year-old Hans Burke stumbled through the door. Knocking the snow from his feet and downing a double brandy, he announced that half a mile down the hill on Broadway, where the railroad trestle passed overhead, cars and trucks were stalled in every direction. Dozens of people were likely to freeze if they didn't get help soon.

Rose Ann reported the problem to the local police.

"We've got a lot of free coffee here—food, too, if it's needed," she told the desk sergeant. "If you can't find anyplace else for them, bring them here. They can sleep on the floor—there's room. Might as well make it a party!"

Her husband, Matt, had called, concerned.

"I'm fine!" she exclaimed. "There's eighteen men here to watch out for me!"

*

A few miles south of Emil's Inn, forty-four-year-old Mary Schmahl and her husband left the Aim Corrugated Container Corporation on Manitoba Street with a few of the ten workers stranded at the company and trudged the block to Riley's Peek Inn Grill on Clinton, north of Seneca. They'd already resigned themselves to spending the night at Aim. Fortunately, the factory had a small kitchen with plenty of food, and the excess carpeting left over from a new decorating job would make several plush mattresses.

To break the monotony, they'd decided to go to the Inn for a few beers. It was crowded and convivial, another New Year's Eve. Mary bought five instant lottery tickets, had a $2 winner and bought two more tickets with the money. Ray Gerwitz, a co-worker at the factory, scraped them for her.

One was a $5,000 winner.

*

That afternoon, a Brinks armored truck traveling south toward the lake bogged down at the end of Washington Street in front of the Buffalo *Evening News* Building. The three guards had just made a series of major pickups and carried more than a dozen bags for weekend storage in the company's vault, but it soon became clear that the truck would be going no farther that day. The guards appealed to the newspaper officials and were told they could store the money in the building.

In the midst of the storm, they loaded the money onto a hand truck, tugged it up and down the snowbanks and, after a twenty-minute effort with comic overtones, reached the building's main entrance, a rotating door: It was frozen shut. The three guards therefore continued to shove and lift the hand truck, laden with an estimated half a million dollars, down the entire length of the block and to the side entrance on Scott Street. They stashed the money in a small room in the building's basement, and from then on two men stood constant guard while the third slept.

*

At McTrevor's Bar, Jeff Hensey was preparing to leave again. Throughout the afternoon, others had dashed out into the storm to loud cheers, only to return hardly a minute later in shivering bewilderment, welcomed back by a chorus of good-natured mocking.

Hensey turned to the girl. She was leaning against the bar, one man's arm around her waist, another's over her shoulder, but he found her eyes were on him, as they had been all afternoon.

"I've got to get going," he told her.

She pulled away from the other men and came to him, a bit unsteady, a slight lisp betraying the half a dozen scotch-and-sodas she'd had.

"What's the big hurry? There ain't nowhere to go and there ain't no way to get there."

That seemed a reasonable argument. Still, he'd had enough to drink—he'd matched her drink for drink, all because of the weather. It seemed he'd endured an eternity of storms and traffic tie-ups, abandoned cars, cancelled plans, tedious and hazardous driving, culminating in the Wednesday night blizzard on the Skyway, those hours of fear verging on panic. And now this insane midday squall that just wouldn't stop. So he'd surrendered, raising not a white flag but the bottom of a scotch on the rocks—six, in fact.

Before the second drink, when he felt she was clinging and on the make, he'd told her, "Look, I'm married, I'm happy and I'm faithful."

"Me, too!" she exclaimed. "My name's Clare—what's yours?"

So he bought her a few drinks, and she insisted on buying him a few. Soon he felt warm, even glowing, and the more severely the snow beat against the windows, the more pleasant his mood became. He told Clare of the Skyway experience, and with his arm around her waist confided that all judges were bastards at heart, even the best of them, for sooner or later they all end up egomaniacs.

She told him she would rather talk about sports.

He remembered making some silly comments about her body, suggesting she try nude modeling. She laughed, but a moment later she walked away and didn't come back for half an hour. He kissed her once, too, and let his hands slip over her hips. And now he was going to leave.

"I've got a brother up on Seneca, near the recreation center."

"So what're you gonna do at your brother's you can't do here?"

"He's got a snowmobile. If he loans it to me I'll drop down to South Park and I'm pretty sure I can get home."

Her face reflected her puzzlement. "What good's that gonna do? You wanna go home?"

It was a good question. His gaze dropped to her breasts, her hips. It was the drink, no doubt. Married six years and he'd never even looked at another woman. Yet, stranded here, with the snow blasting the windowpanes, something was changing inside him.

"I gotta go," he said, lifting his coat from the stool.

"Well, I might as well go with you," she said. "My folks live out that way, not far from the center. Might as well walk together— you're so damn drunk you'll pass out and never get home."

He shrugged, and finally smiled.

"Okay, Clare," he said. "It's you and me against the world." He pulled her hat down tight over her ears, lifted her collar, tied the scarf snugly around her neck. She did the same for him and, with boots jangling, they stomped to the doorway. The crowd cheered them.

"Lucky sonofabitch," somebody shouted. In the spirit of things, Jeff waved farewell.

"They'll be back," someone said.

*

With darkness, tension spread through the city. All afternoon shoppers and workers by the thousands had gathered to wait out the storm. They'd congregated in hallways and offices, lobbies of tall buildings, stores, restaurants, bars, the courthouse, the post office. Early that evening, Hotel Statler owner Robert Zugger reported all 400 rooms rented (many to Ed Janak of DOT, to house state workers coming to the city), an additional 400 cots set up in hallways and meeting rooms. All afternoon the hotel had served free coffee in the crowded lobby. With night approaching, the management had moved television sets into the ballrooms.

The overflow was the same at the Holiday Inn on Delaware Avenue and the Howard Johnson's Motor Lodge on Dingens Street, the Executive Motor Inn on Genesee, the Lafayette on Washington and Court.

Crowds thronged police and fire stations, and more than three hundred stumbled into the Memorial Auditorium near the Skyway. Joseph Figliola, manager of the auditorium, served free coffee and soup, and passed out basketballs to the youngsters.

Another 200 who had been shopping at the Main Place Mall crossed a covered pedestrian bridge to the Rath Building, where they would spend the night. Seven hundred were stranded at the Donovan State Office Building.

While some establishments insisted on closing and ordered the stranded out into the storm, others welcomed them. One of those was Hengerer's Department Store on Main Street, diagonally across from the Lafayette Hotel. By five o'clock, the store's management realized that its restaurant would be feeding a great many people that night: stranded workers from the Niagara Mohawk Power Company's skyscraper a few blocks away, employees of National Fuel Gas in the Rand Building next door, as well as its own snowbound customers and workers. Hengerer's geared up to feed three dinner shifts, and within the next two hours served 1,000 people.

It was obvious that most of them would have to remain overnight or risk freezing to death on the streets, for radio reports indicated that no transportation existed, the city was paralyzed and the winds had reached hurricane force, with a windchill factor now approaching 70 below zero. About a third of the store personnel started making plans to distribute bedding, blankets, pillows and towels, not only to those at the store, but also to the gas and electric companies. They set up a dormitory arrangement: The fifth and seventh floors would house the women; the sixth, the men. Workers distributed toothbrushes and toothpaste. The restaurant began preparing for 1,000 breakfast guests the next morning, while another crew handled takeout orders throughout the night.

Early in the evening, executives of the Hengerer Company made a simple policy decision: No one would be charged a cent for food or bedding. After the emergency, the twenty thousand dollars' worth of used blankets, sheets, towels and such would be donated to the Salvation Army.

All over the city, churches, stores and private citizens threw open their doors to the pummeled and bedraggled in need of food and shelter. Said Father Hubert Reimann, pastor of St. Jude's Church in Sardinia, a Buffalo suburb, "We'll take care of each other, and we'll get through."

In every bar in the downtown area people congregated in jovial and sensual inebriation.

*

A man walked into a snowmobile dealer's store on South Park, pointed to a machine and asked, "How much does this cost?" He picked up a helmet, suit and boots, changed into them, laid $2,000 in cash on the counter, and drove off in his new vehicle.

*

Earlier in the day David Kelly, the mayor's confidential aide, had announced that City Hall would remain open all night. "We've opened the cafeteria on a twenty-four-hour basis," he said. "They've got food—I'm not sure how long it will last, but they do have supplies down there. We've been in touch with the Red Cross, and they're bringing cots and blankets. And we're working now to locate anyone in the building who needs special medical treatment so we can get them in one place and get whatever they need."

Although people were free to leave if they wished, Kelly said, "We're advising against it. Right now, the best thing anyone can do is stay put."

The most pressing concern among the more than six hundred spending the night at City Hall seemed to be that they'd miss the evening's TV hit miniseries *Roots*. As early as 5:30, people began crowding into the office of Robert C. Penn, the Human Resources Commissioner. His was City Hall's most glamorous office, and included a color TV.

Others decided upon an all-night card game. Most of the building's twenty-four floors could boast at least one game, complete with smoke-filled room and liquor delivered regularly from a liquor store across the square.

On the second floor, Mayor Stanley Makowski lifted a blind and peered into the oppressive whiteness. With a shudder, he turned quickly away and faced the remnants of staff able to answer his summons for a strategy meeting. The reports since noon continued to grow more troublesome. James Lindner announced that both DOT's and city's snow-removal equipment was at a standstill—the snow was blowing so hard that the drivers couldn't see to avoid stalled cars and the occasional foolhardy pedestrian who might step into their path. The police commissioner had equally fearful news: The entire bureau was in chaos. Headquarters was operating on a skeleton crew left over from the earlier shift. Precinct 7 was snowbound. So were a few others. None of the city's forty-five cruisers had snow chains, and the thirteen sets the city owned were locked in a storage room at the Seneca Street Garage—but no one was quite sure who had the key to the lock. Police Commissioner Thomas Blair had authorized officers to buy chains from any store they could find open, but by then the cruisers were already bogged down or buried, and virtually the entire police force was immobile.

Yet calls for help were overwhelming the radio room staff. Many elderly were without food, some without heat; hundreds of people might be stranded on streets and highways, and there had been a few calls from diabetics who had run out of insulin.

An aide suggested that, through radio and TV bulletins, the public could be apprised of the situation and asked to loan their snowmobiles and four-wheel-drive vehicles to the police department. Within an hour, the pleas were being broadcast.

Police Commissioner Blair also asked the Erie County React, a group of citizens' band radio operators, to continually broadcast the department's need for snowmobiles to patrol Fuhrmann Boulevard and rescue hundreds of stranded motorists.

Bob Rung, Director of General Services at City Hall, predicted that, with stragglers still coming in, the building would have to accommodate about seven hundred guests for the night. Space was no problem, although most of the people would end up sleeping on the floor. But some hadn't had a meal since breakfast, and almost none had eaten dinner—yet the cafeteria was about out of food. If everyone would go home in the morning, the throng could weather a night of hunger. But there was little chance the storm would break.

"I got news," a maintenance man announced. "Some of them damn old pipes in the basement musta froze up, 'cause they cracked and there's water all over the place."

The mayor grew pale. "We can't panic," he muttered. "We mustn't panic."

Bob Rung volunteered to handle the food problem. When the meeting adjourned, he called Al Nowiki, Superintendent of the Delaware Park Labor Center.

*

Delaware Avenue begins at Niagara Square and City Hall, extends north to Gates Circle and the Millard Fillmore Hospital and beyond that to an exclusive area of parks, golf courses, cemeteries and college campuses. There, in Delaware Park, it passes beneath the Scajaquada Expressway. At that junction is the Delaware Park Labor Center.

Twenty-six-year-old mechanic Mark DuMond sat in the city tow truck at the Labor Center lot and watched a Cadillac come off the Expressway and down an exit ramp. The car's front right tire had gone flat, and long before it reached the intersection at the bottom, DuMond realized the vehicle would not proceed through the accumulating snow. In fact, it stopped abruptly, and the car behind it skidded like a sled for twenty feet before hitting the Cadillac's rear bumper.

During the next few minutes, one car after another came off the exit ramp to become entangled in the maze.

Mark DuMond sighed. He'd spent a long week towing stranded and abandoned cars so that the city's plows could get through and clean the streets, and when not driving he'd helped repair and service damaged equipment at the garage. Today, he'd not even had time for lunch. Although the snow hadn't blown as heavily this far north, driving had still been tedious, particularly because increased visibility encouraged more drivers onto the roads, producing more tie-ups and traffic accidents. Mark had spent most of the day towing cars like the Cadillac out of intersections to make way for the plows. He was tired and hungry, and wanted to go home. But Al Nowiki, the superintendent in charge, had already told him he'd have to work a second shift. He'd agreed without complaint—he'd seen enough throughout the day to know he'd never get home anyway.

With mild disgust, Mark pulled the tow truck into the intersection, spun it around and backed toward the Caddy.

Not until 7 P M did he find time to return to the garage for a sandwich and a hot cup of coffee. He was sitting at the table in the locker room relaxing with Angelo Pintabowa and Al Hoffman when Superintendent Nowiki came into the room.

"Just got a call," said the tall, white-haired Nowiki. "Looks like we're getting important or somethin'—it was Bob Rung *himself* down there at City Hall, right under the mayor."

None of the three at the table showed enthusiasm. It could only mean more work, no matter where the order originated.

"Seems they got a hell of a lot of people stranded. What they want us to do . . ." Nowiki was an aggressive, hard-driving boss, not given to hesitation. Yet, now he took a deep breath.

"They need food," he said finally, "or there's gonna be about seven hundred hungry people down there. I want you to get the bus going, take it over to that TOPS Market down there on Niagara. Let 'em load it for you, and get it to City Hall. Get started now."

"We're eatin' supper."

"Well get *done* eating supper and then get *started*."

It wasn't until Nowiki left the room that one of the men said, "He's gotta be nuts—you couldn't get a tank through some of them streets, much less that junk pile he calls a bus."

"The damn thing won't even start, don't worry."

"Look," said Mark, "Al and I'll take the tow truck and Angelo, you handle the bus. That way, if the heap breaks down, Al and I'll get back safe and it's no big loss.

"Sure, sure," said Pintabowa dryly.

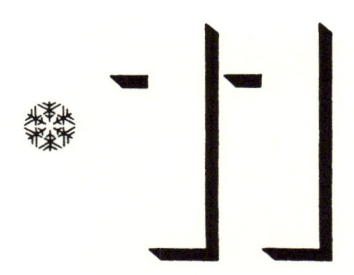

It was 5:31 PM at Chef's Restaurant, and Bill Strobele was helping Lou Billittier stuff towels in the exhaust fans over the grill to prevent the snow from blowing in, when the electricity failed. Immediately the battery-operated emergency lights flashed on, creating a prison-yard atmosphere of glaring light and contrasting darkness.

Breaking into the line at the phone booth, Lou dialed the number of the wax factory a few blocks away. A moment later he went to the kitchen.

"I want an urn full of coffee over to the wax factory right away," he told an assistant. "Take as many guys as you need. They're paying in candles. Yeah, you heard me—candles. Two cases of 'em. We need *atmosphere* in this place!"

Strobele slipped into his insulated vest, boots and coat. Again he refused Lou's offer of a double brandy for the road—he'd been through 30-below-zero winters in Korea while serving there, he said, and he'd learned then that alcohol and exertion in cold temperatures don't mix.

"Well, have a meal, at least, for God's sake. You don't know when you'll get the next one, once they put you to work down there."

"I appreciate it, but I got my lunch." He held up the plastic bag. "I'll be back for that free drink in the spring, though," he said, and stepped out into the blizzard.

It was as though death had descended upon the city. In all the expanse of Seneca Street there was no life, only the animal howl of

73

the wind. The temperature had dropped even further—a thermometer on a factory Bill passed indicating minus 7 degrees. He estimated that the more violent gusts were reaching seventy-five miles per hour, and at such moments, with progress impossible, he would retreat into a hallway, cringe behind a snow-buried car or huddle on the downwind side of a telephone pole. Often he turned and walked backwards into the wind, sparing his face, now virtually hidden in the scarf.

Two blocks from Chef's, near Michigan Avenue, a flash brightened the night. To his right, in an open field, a wire danced crazily across the snow, its tip glowing like a Fourth of July sparkler, occasionally bursting into a shower of brilliance. Above it, on the pole, the driving snow sizzled against an overheating transformer and melted, the water streaming to the ground to form a mound of ice. Bill memorized the location—between Michigan and a small alley called Butler Place on Myrtle Avenue, a block north of Seneca. That was the source of the power failure at the restaurant. He would report it when he reached headquarters.

The journey along Seneca Street continued to grow more difficult, and finally Bill turned into an alley and caught his breath, then proceeded north to Swann, where houses broke the wind's attack. Following Swann toward the lake, he came to Oak, where a tractor trailer had blocked the intersection, trapping two buses. They were empty now, their passengers crowded into the Major Hooper's Restaurant on the corner. In the next block, he passed several more stranded and empty buses.

In all that journey, he came upon only two other pedestrians. A well-dressed young man and an attractive woman dashed laughing from McTrevor's bar at Washington and Swann, almost colliding with him.

"I beg your pardon," said the man with a bow. "Lovely day."

*

At Pearl Street, two blocks from Headquarters, where the sweep from the lake is uninterrupted by tall buildings and the wind rolls summer and winter over the land with great force, Bill encountered the most devastating wind of all. He clung to the steel rails architects had designed along their buildings' plazas for such purposes, then inched along, grasping car-door handles, moving tortuously from vehicle to vehicle. Finally a building on the far corner of Franklin Street offered some protection, and from there he proceeded quickly to the station.

He punched in at twenty-five minutes after six. It had taken five and a half hours to get to work. Three day-shift dispatchers—Fred Hook, Dan Alian and Tom Walters—greeted him in the radio room with feeble smiles that spoke of their fatigue. It was not merely the few hours of overtime that had exhausted them, but the incredible volume of work: When not on the radio, the dispatchers had been answering 911 calls because many of the operators hadn't made it to work.

Strobele took over immediately. The desk he confronted that night was entirely covered with stacks of complaint cards, perhaps two dozen piles with thirty to fifty cards in each. All were waiting to be sent to officers in the field, typically about forty-five cruisers and auxiliary vehicles blanketing the city. But tonight, Strobele had been told, every one of those vehicles was snowbound, most abandoned, and the few officers that had reported to work were making their own rules, relying on ingenuity and initiative. Some had reported to the precinct nearest their homes, rather than waste the night trying to get to their regular beats.

Officer Patrick O'Brien's cruiser had finally bogged down on South Park, so he and his partner went to work right there, leading passengers from stranded buses to churches and warehouses where they could keep warm and telephone worried relatives.

Assured that no motorists remained in their cars, O'Brien called Strobele to announce formation of his own foot patrol. Strobele gave him his first assignment—to bring five dozen rolls from a nearby bakery to the two hundred hungry people on the first floor of Police Headquarters.

Officer William Cooley called in from the Seneca Street firehouse where Strobele had stopped a couple of hours earlier to report that he was unable to reach his precinct, but had borrowed a snowmobile and would answer all calls for emergency medical supplies and food for precincts 7, 9 and 15. He'd call in from wherever he happened to be, after completing each assignment, to pick up a new one.

Only a fraction of the complaints received answers, for by then not more than half a dozen private citizens had volunteered snowmobiles and four-wheel drive vehicles for police use. Those were sent on only the most crucial missions—rescuing the stranded, delivering essential drugs, transporting patients to hospitals, bringing food to the hungry.

Other callers were directed to private agencies. Operators at

911 offered simple advice and information—which food stores planned to remain open all night, where emergency shelters had been established, symptoms of frostbite and how to treat it, when and where to seek medical help.

At the first opportunity, Strobele called the Niagara Mohawk Electric Company Service Department.

"That power failure on Seneca Street," he said, "I think I know where the problem is." He described the downed wire, the location of the transformer.

"Well that saves us about a day's work just knowing where it is," said the spokesman. "But we're still not gonna get there for three or four days—some of the roads down there—why, there *aren't* any. They're just wiped off the map, car roofs sticking up, and that's it."

"Look, you get your equipment dug out and ready to move," said Bill. "People are gonna freeze without their oil burners firing soon—and that takes electricity. You get the equipment out—I'll get you a path to the wire."

Piecing together reports from the handful of volunteer mobile units and others that had come in throughout the day, he determined which of the city's major streets were still navigable. Michigan Avenue appeared the only possibility from the Niagara Mohawk facilities to the downed line on Myrtle Avenue. Still, drifts and monumental traffic tie-ups north of Swann, a few blocks from Myrtle, seemed an insurmountable obstacle.

Strobele called the Seneca Street Garage. "We need the tow truck near Michigan and Swann," he told the officer who answered. But the power failure had affected the garage, too. The massive motorized steel door could not be opened and the tow truck was trapped inside.

"We're hanging by our teeth from the roof," said the officer at the garage, "chipping the goddamn ice away with chisels and hammers, and there's guys with their hands bleeding, but we'll have the lousy door open in an hour."

Someone handed Strobele an item from the teletype machine. He shrugged and smiled wryly. Maybe he didn't have it so bad after all. At that moment, a state police officer on Route 31 near Albion, New York, was filling out an accident report involving 50 cars and 115 people.

12

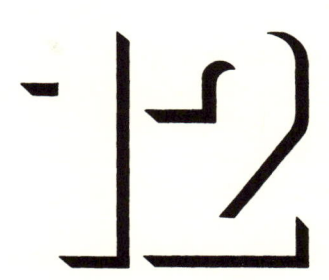

During supper at the Falzone house on Whitney Place that night, young Joe Paul entertained his parents and twin sisters, sixteen-year-old Beverly and Barbara, with stories of his day at the Berge Wallpaper Company.

"You guys don't know how the other half lives, hiding in that store all day," he joked with his parents. "You think a catastrophe's a leaky milk carton!"

At 7 PM, Joe Falzone turned on the television. He and the girls settled into the sofa to watch *Roots*. Joe Paul brought out his new camera, a 34-mm Konika, knelt in front of the fifty-gallon fish tank in the dining room and focused on a blue fantail. Joe's wife, Laura, was resting. The wind howled past the window.

Someone hammered on the door, and Laura roused herself with a groan to answer it. The pounding grew more persistent.

"I'm coming, I'm coming, for goodness' sake." At the door stood Juan Rivera, a young neighbor, breathless and wide-eyed.

"You gotta get outta here, quick—next door's on fire!" he called. In the living room, Joe Senior thought he'd heard the boy say, "The store's on fire," and with the agility of a man many years younger, he slipped into his boots, threw on his coat and gloves and hurried out the door and toward the store. Joe Paul followed but, upon reaching the street, turned left to the neighbor's house. After a few steps, he saw the glow, the rich orange of a sunset, defused now through the almost opaque curtain of snow. Yet Joe Paul could distinguish the flames reaching the rear walls and roof of the adjoining house, and their heat drove away the cold and warmed him.

His neighbors milled in the street.

"My God, there's three kids in that apartment!" Joe Paul shouted.

"They're all right," someone replied.

"The big black guy in the front flat rescued 'em all. Lucky, huh?"

According to the neighbors, a mother had left her three children in the care of an older child while she went out for a time. When the apartment grew uncomfortably cold, the five-year-old threw a newspaper into the oven to make more heat. When the paper burst into flame, the child, frightened, withdrew it, and when it scorched his hand, he threw it onto the bed.

Running back to the house, Joe Paul told his mother to call the fire department.

Joe Senior came back in. "The store's not on fire," he said.

"It's next door—*next door!* Look, the wind's whipping it and it's burning like hell. If there's anything you want to save, you better get it now and get out, 'cause this house is gonna burn."

Disbelief came to Laura Falzone's face. She turned to Joe Senior.

"Don't worry, the fire department'll be here in a minute," he assured her. "But no sense taking chances—let's get what we can and pack it in the van. Come on!"

Through driving snow and hip-high drifts, the Falzones carried the microwave oven, a few pieces of expensive crystal, a leather jacket to the van. Barbara Falzone rescued her gerbils. Someone remembered the dog. Half a dozen neighbors—blacks, Puerto Ricans and whites, the Whitney Place neighborhood—offered help.

Joe Paul pulled an armload of shirts from the closet and tossed them in a basket.

"You're gonna *wrinkle* them!" Laura scolded. "I just ironed them all!" He gazed at her patiently. She shook her head and wept.

During the next fifteen minutes, the Falzones called the fire department twice more. Although they'd heard the scream of sirens, the sounds seemed to come from great distances, and not to grow closer.

Within half an hour after Juan Rivera had warned them of the fire, the Falzone house was in flames. By 8:15, it was destroyed. From a bar on the corner across from the grocery store, Joe Paul watched as hurricane-force winds hurled blazing timbers over the roofs of houses half a block from the blaze. Windows across the street burst from the heat, and water from melting snow swamped the intersection and froze.

The house separating the Falzone rubble from the grocery store on the corner began to burn. Flying timber ignited the rear porch of the building next to the store on Virginia Avenue. The store stood like an island in a sea of flames.

The blinking neon light on the beer sign bathed the snow in front of the bar in alternating blue and red. The colors were reflected in Joe Paul's eyes. He was not religious; yet he prayed. The store was his parents' whole life. The house was a great loss, but they could survive. But if the store burned, it would kill them.

In the van across the street, bathed in the fire's brightness, his mother and sisters clung together, Barbara with the gerbil cage on her lap. He wondered if his mother had found shoes or slippers. She'd left the house in such confusion she hadn't realized until several minutes after reaching the van that she'd no more than a pair of stockings on her feet.

In the course of a single hour they'd lost their home, he thought, and in the next, their whole lives might fall apart. He was not ashamed of the tears that flickered in blue and red on his face.

*

For the Buffalo Fire Department, as for virtually everyone else in the city, the day had been a microcosm of the entire winter. In the morning, an exhausted crew had continued the endless chore of locating fire hydrants beneath the snow and shoveling them clear. Firefighters had been called to help repair broken water mains, give emergency aid, extinguish small fires and answer the day's four dozen false alarms.

Fatigue and illness had left the fire department severely undermanned. Earlier in the season, ten of the city's thirty-two firehouses had closed and personnel had been shifted to other strategic stations to provide full teams. Fortunately, the day of the blizzard, many of the day shift personnel stayed on duty for an extra shift, and the trucks that were running had the required minimum crew of four men.

At 7:53 PM, the first signal flashed in the windowless third-floor alarm room at 332 Ellicott Street. It was a Preliminary Signal from a firebox on the corner of Whitney Place and Carolina Street, a block south of Virginia, the caller reporting merely a suspicion of fire—the smell of smoke. He was unsure of the location. Thus, the dispatcher, Chief Jerry Sullivan, ordered out half the equipment usually sent to a one-alarm fire: two pump trucks and one ladder. Sullivan's call was to the Tupper and Washington Station for pump engine 9 and hook and ladder 1. It was not the nearest station, six blocks from the fire—there was another two blocks closer at Jersey Street and Plymouth Avenue. But snow and stalled cars had utterly isolated it from the rest of the city.

Engine 13, just behind City Hall on Court Street, was also within a few blocks, but had been dispatched to another alarm. So, under Sullivan's orders, engine 1, from South Division and Ellicott, a block north and east of McTrevor's Bar, set out for Whitney Place.

Three minutes later, Sullivan learned the exact location of the Whitney Place fire—Laura Falzone was on the phone giving what details she could. Immediately he called out two more pumpers and another ladder.

When the first call reached the Tupper and Washington firehouse, engine 9 was on the road with a television crew shooting network news footage of what promised to be the most punishing storm of a record-breaking winter.

When the call reached engine 9, it was a mere four blocks from the fire. Twenty minutes later, it was still half a block from the hydrant at Virginia and Whitney. The driver at the wheel literally plowed his way through the impossible maze, ramming stalled cars out of his path, plunging into great mounds of snow to bypass others. Neighborhood people cheered it on, and when the engine lost traction they kicked the snow from its path and threw their weight against the great machine to inch it forward.

Meanwhile, Captain Phil Morana and his chief, coming from another direction, had bogged down three blocks from the fire. Carrying a portable radio, Morana trudged two blocks until, against an orange sky, he saw the silhouette of engine 9 and the mass of people pushing it through the snow. They were in the intersection now, preparing to run hoses.

Moving closer, Morana counted two houses ablaze, the wind-driven flames arching thirty feet into the air. The street was alight with the shower of glowing embers, and flaming timbers and boards hailed upon roofs several blocks away. Some tumbled onto the roof of the store on the corner.

Deciding not to waste time trying to make a closer inspection, Morana shielded the radio from the wind and called the Alarm

Room. Using his chief's signature, he asked for a second alarm. It would bring three more trucks and two more ladders.

Nine minutes later, while Morana joined the neighbors and firemen of engine 9 dragging the hoses through the snow toward the blaze, Chief Jerry Sullivan activated a third alarm. Now, eleven engines and seven trucks proceeded against impossible odds toward Whitney Place.

Engine 4 attempted the journey from South Buffalo, made it as far as the Fillmore tie-up, the one Bill Strobele had walked around on Seneca, turned north into Smith and was blocked by twelve cars.

Engine 35 stalled in a jam of thirty cars and buses. By then, the fire had engulfed a fourth house.

While his mother and sisters, the gerbils and the dog huddled in the van and Joe Senior assisted the firemen, young Joe Paul watched the confusion in the intersection. Almost an hour had passed since the fire first broke out, and still engine 9 and its crew struggled alone against the blaze. Firemen had connected the heavy two-and-a-half-inch hose to the hydrant on the corner and, while neighbors stomped a path through the drifts and helped to uncoil the lengths of line, the firemen dragged it inch by inch toward the fire. Finally, when they reached the flames, the hose expanded in a surge of water, snaking across the snow. From its nozzle the stream arched into the driving wind, dropping with little effect onto the swirling fire.

At that moment, an army of firefighters and volunteers struggled toward Whitney Place from every direction, snaking at least ten hoses two and three blocks across car roofs and backyard fences, through alleys and over drifts. Joe Paul watched as, with what seemed like eternal slowness, they strained toward the intersection, sinking into the freezing slush from the runoff of the engine 9 hose, many dropping away in pain or exhaustion, others hurrying to fill their places.

Through the intersection the leaders proceeded like an advancing infantry, the brass nozzle of the hose their banner. The slush quickly froze on the hose, adding to its weight. It flowed over the men's boots, impaired their footing. Still, shouting encouragement to each other, they lurched forward.

On the twenty-fourth floor of City Hall, Fire Commissioner Karl Kubiak listened intently to the jumble of reports over the fire radio—apparatus stranded all over the city, fewer than half the hoses and men needed to fight the blaze on Whitney Place, the fire spreading. He'd already ordered up the Civil Defense Auxiliary Fire

Corps and called back all off-duty men. But now he realized he needed outside help—was it Morana who had said he wouldn't be surprised if the whole city burned?

A moment later, Commissioner Kubiak was on the phone asking the National Guard to open up the streets around Virginia and Whitney at any cost.

Lieutenant Colonel Gerald Harris couldn't give an immediate answer, for, according to the plan established that morning, all Guard assignments had to come directly from DOT disaster coordinator Ed Janak.

At that moment, Janak was in the lobby of the Statler Hotel with other DOT employees. In the past few hours he'd grown starkly aware of the awesome responsibility that had befallen him. The city had been overwhelmed by an immediate crisis such as it had never known. The potential for tragedy was everywhere, and the ultimate responsibility for preventing full scale devastation rested with Janak himself.

The pocket radio Lindner had given him that morning crackled. It was Colonel Harris of the National Guard, but Janak couldn't even understand who he was trying to reach—perhaps there was too great a distance between the hotel and the armory, or perhaps the weather was interfering with the signal. The static continued for several minutes. Finally, another voice—it might have been Lindner's deputy—responded with a clear signal. "Look, if anybody knows where the hell Janak is, get him in touch with Harris right away. The Guard's gotta job to do and they need his okay."

*

Even the National Guard equipment couldn't perform miracles—the distance from the armory to Whitney Place was too far and the snow too deep. Instead, using four-wheel drives, the guards picked up firemen at firehouses all over the city and ferried them to Whitney Place. Fire Commissioner Kubiak repeatedly requested radio and TV stations to urge off-duty firemen to go to the firehouses nearest their homes and await the Guard.

Kubiak also ordered an entire block of houses near the fire evacuated. Hundreds of people in the neighborhood rushed into the streets ill-dressed for the storm.

Through the binding snow they stumbled, many confused and lost. Children became separated from their parents. Some, seeking warmth, moved toward the fire, cluttering the area. An elderly man wandered aimlessly along Elmwood Avenue.

Some teenage boys found him and took him to their place, the Buffalo Home for Delinquent and Troubled Youth. They gave him food and a bed, then went out again to find evacuees and guide them to shelter. They led many to Father David's Holy Cross Rectory and gymnasium on Niagara Street, a few blocks west of the fire. They guided a dozen frostbitten children to nearby Columbus Hospital. Throughout the night, the bewildered processions trudged west into the blizzard, the boys pausing for a cup of coffee and a moment's warmth, then returning to Whitney Place to guide another group.

The Spanish-American Alliance offered its facilities as field headquarters for the firemen. Others took refuge in a neighborhood bar, the Ultima Cupa—the Last Cup.

From the bar, Joe Paul saw a flurry of activity near the burned ruins that had been his neighbor's house. Firemen gestured and dropped the hose. Others ran toward the spot. Tightening his scarf, Joe Paul hurried out of the bar and across the now ice-caked intersection. As he approached the fire, he heard someone say that a fireman had fallen through weak timbers into a basement, breaking his leg. The others were grimly fighting back the flames and struggling to free him before other timbers fell. In a moment the man was free, and Joe Paul helped lift him, leading the men to his father's van. Half an hour later, an ambulance crew arrived carrying a stretcher. They had come on foot from Columbus Hospital at Carolina and Niagara, three blocks away. They paused only a minute to warm their hands, then loaded the injured firemen onto the stretcher and trudged off.

Joe Paul stood beside the grocery store gazing up into the flames, his coat open, his face stinging with the heat. "We could use twice the equipment we have," one of the firemen had said moments earlier. "But, Christ, what we really need is men. I mean, trained men. This storm, it's a killer. We can't take any more."

By then, it was apparent to the firemen that at least five houses on Whitney, three on Virginia and the Falzone grocery store on the corner would be destroyed. Everything was going wrong. When they shut off one hose to move it, the water inside it promptly froze, bursting it. When they patched the broken section, they found the nozzle had frozen. And when the runoff water froze on the street, it trapped hoses beneath a foot of ice. The firemen had to use jackhammers to free them.

Three pumpers stalled when the wind drove snow onto the motors. Since the equipment is always kept in heated garages or running when on the road, the department never used antifreeze in the radiators, and now, within an hour, the water in the engines froze, expanded and split the engines.

Against such odds the men continued to fight. One wept. Another, a few feet from Joe Paul knelt in the snow praying.

PART II

In wondrous ways do the gods make sport with men. — Titus Maccius Plautus

13

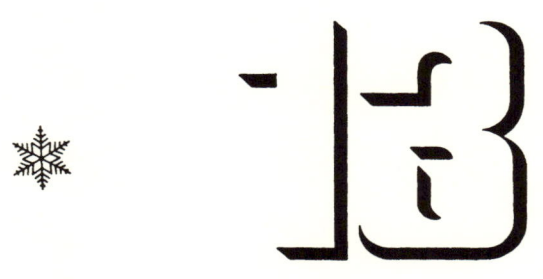

Fifty million square miles of the earth's surface is perpetually under the dominion of snow. On a cold, windless day, there will accumulate on every two-square-foot patch of Buffalo rooftop or Siberian rock face or Greenland floe more than a million snow crystals for every ten inches of snow. Multiplied by those fifty million square miles of snow blanket, and by the varying depths, snow crystals rival in number the earth's grains of sand, its individual insects and higher animal life; snow is among the most populous of kingdoms.

It is also among the oldest, for it was there in the beginning, in the darkness, falling upon the deep, three to five billion years before the first algae, the first bacteria, found nurture in its thawing.

They are individuals—the snow crystals, for although most are six-sided, some have three and others five surfaces. Beyond that, the Russian meteorologist Shuchukevich discovered 246 different kinds of crystals in 1910, and there are probably a great many more: hexagons, needles, hollow prismatic columns, fernlike stars. At freezing, the crystals fuse, creating snowflakes. In the wind, they beat against each other, sanding themselves smooth and taking on the shape of planets.

The language of Eskimos distinguishes two dozen or more kinds of snow—the windblown, the new-fallen, soft snow, fluffy deep snow, wind-packed snow, wet springtime snow, cold, crusted snow, dry and sugary snow, drifted, rounded, gently sloping snows.

In the winter of 1970–71, more than eighty-six feet of snow fell in Paradise, Washington, setting the United States seasonal accumulation record. Tamarack, California, near Lake Tahoe, was buried under 390 inches of snow in the single month of January 1911. In one storm, from February 13 to 19, 1959, 189 inches of snow fell in northern California. In a single day in April 1921, snow 76 inches deep covered Silver Lake, Colorado.

Some creatures perish in the cold and snow; some endure. Others, like the white bear, armed with blades of teeth and claw, skin oily and waterproof, olfactory sense keen and dependable through the long night, flourish and are at home.

*

As the wolf pack is drawn to the weak and fallen prey, and the shark grows frenzied at the scent of blood, the prowlers, learning through the City Hall's bulletins that the blizzard had completely immobilized the police department, began stalking the empty city. Some smashed cigarette and soft drink and milk machines. Others stripped abandoned vehicles. In the Justine Avenue and Williams Street section, and on South Park near the snowbound seventh precinct, the looting was most serious. There, drivers from the closed thruway had parked long lines of trucks, and vehicle after vehicle was systematically ransacked. At some point during the blizzard, thieves heisted six thousand dollars' worth of coffee from one semi-truck, four hundred pounds of meat from another, an entire load of refrigerators from a third. A beer truck was emptied.

Looters hit factories, homes and stores. Sofas and beds disappeared across the snow, and even a few cars, left buried to their windshields in snow and trapped in a maze of other stranded vehicles, were somehow stolen.

The looters stalked the Whitney Place neighborhood, too. While the sky was still bright with flames, they ransacked abandoned firetrucks, broke open the lockers and stole firefighters' clothing, disconnected radios, severed nozzles from their hozes for their value as scrap brass.

Jeff Hensey and the girl watched the feathery images glide silently across the landscape, their arms filled with packages. He counted six of them, three moving from the shattered store window to the jeep, three back to the store. Now a flurry of snow swept them into oblivion.

"And at a time like this!" said Clare.

14

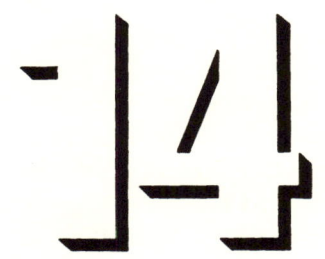

At 10 P M , the silence of Niagara Square was broken by the muffled rumble of an engine. The headlights of a bus broke through the snow as though it were opaque glass, the vehicle lumbered around two stalled cars and stopped at a 45-degree angle in front of City Hall. The door opened and fifty people dashed through the building.

"Been in that goddamn thing since two o'clock this afternoon!" someone told the police officer at the door. "Two and a half miles in eight hours!"

On the building's second floor, a hysterical woman screamed for a doctor. Someone called the fire commissioner's office on the twenty-fourth floor, and he sent two firemen to help. In the elevator, one of the two agreed to be the doctor. He found the woman in a state of anxiety-produced panic, examined her eyes and ears, took her pulse while mumbling, "Yes, of course. Okay." With somber authority he prescribed a glass of cold water.

"That'll do it," he assured her. "You'll be just fine." She recovered immediately.

On the second floor, Mayor Stanley Makowski was on the phone pleading with an aide to the governor, trying to explain calmly and in believable terms the extent to which the city had been crippled and his concern that the storm still showed no sign of ending. Hour after hour, in what might have been the coldest office in the entire building, Makowski had been making telephone calls: Toronto agreed to send assistance; so did New York City. Finally, even someone on the President's staff in Washington agreed to an investigation.

An aide reminded the mayor that feeding the fifty who had come in from the bus had all but depleted the cafeteria's dwindling food supply, and most of the hundreds who were stranded in the building still hadn't eaten. Now, some were complaining of hunger. Bob Rung assured the mayor that the bus had already left the Delaware Park Labor Center, and was expected any moment at City Hall, loaded with enough food to feed an army.

*

Mark DuMond of the Delaware Park Labor Center stood in the snow with Angelo Pintabowa and Al Hoffman and stared at the old yellow school bus with patient indifference. It was a '68 Ford, bruised and battered into retirement years earlier, resurrected to transport senior citizens to occasional city-sponsored programs, but spending more time lately at the garage undergoing repairs than transporting the elderly. Its most recent ailment had been cured only a few days earlier, and now it languished half buried in a snowbank.

Someone had left the bus door wide open, and the snowbank that had begun outside the bus continued building inside it, burying the driver's seat and much of the front passenger section. The three men uttered some casual profanity, argued about who was responsible for leaving the door open, debated how to go about removing the snow and finally agreed that the first step should be another round of hot coffee.

Some time later, the trio attempted to shovel a path to the driver's seat, but the effort proved futile—each shovel of snow thrown out the door was immediately blown back into the men's faces. They considered throwing the snow further back into the bus, but fresh snow continued replacing it. Someone suggested they close the door, and after clearing the snow away from the steps, they attempted to do so, but the door-closing apparatus had frozen.

"Let's just drive the damn thing into the garage and let it thaw out," Mark said. But the engine wouldn't start, soaked as it was with snow, and finally the battery went dead. So Mark started the tow truck, a titan of a vehicle used to haul the city's ten-ton dump and trash collecting vehicles, and dragged the bus inside.

By 11 PM, the men had replaced the battery, dried the engine, shoveled out the snow and thawed the door-closing mechanism. After innumerable attempts, the old engine kicked over, and with Angelo Pintabowa at the wheel, it creaked backwards and out into the snow. A moment later the tow truck, with Mark DuMond at the wheel and Al Hoffman in the passenger seat, broke a path toward the Scajaquada Expressway and proceeded southwest to Main Street.

*

Major Bob Williams gazed out the front window of the Salvation Army Headquarters on North Main Street to see yet another person stumbling toward the building. Forcing the heavy glass door open against the wind, he welcomed to the fold the forty-ninth sheep.

They'd been arriving since three o'clock that afternoon, most of them having abandoned their cars in the impassable drifts to wander blindly in search of any shelter. Later, some arrived on fire trucks and a four-wheel-drive vehicle the police had commandeered. By then, the Salvation Army's phones had begun an incessant jangling—people by the scores called for food, rescue, drugs, fuel, advice, consultation, prayer. Captain Geof Banfield set up a command post at the reception desk in the Golden Age Club wing, recruiting a few assistants to help him answer the phones, while Major Bob Williams assumed the food detail. He set one crew to work preparing dinner for the fifty-five people already at the center, and led another group across the street to Bell's Market, where he purchased a great quantity of food on credit. Back at the center, he organized eight assistants into sandwich-making assembly lines. Shopping bags of food waiting for delivery soon extended the entire 150 feet of the Golden Age Club hall.

Another crew made enough coffee to fill eighteen 10-gallon urns. Captain Banfield notified the police and fire departments that food and supplies were ready to go to churches, police stations, firehouses and anywhere else they were needed—but the Salvation Army itself didn't have the means to get it there. Soon, volunteers arrived in snowmobiles and four-wheel drives, and within a few hours a transport team of about thirty filled the last link in a simple but extremely efficient system: Banfield and his crew, receiving telephone requests, passed them in writing to Williams, whose helpers filled the orders and numbered each package, writing the same number on the request slip. A volunteer took the slip with the name and address to which a delivery was to be made, found the corresponding package among the hundreds numerically stacked along the corridor, and set out on his next delivery. Thus, a few thousand dollars' worth of food was dispersed every forty-five minutes.

With every telephone line jammed and people standing in line to use the phones, one staff member recalled the ham radio setup in the adjoining building. The expensive equipment had been purchased ten years earlier for just such an emergency as this, so that even with telephone lines down or overburdened, radio-equipped field workers could still communicate with headquarters. In all those years it had remained idle because an emergency requiring it had never materialized. Now, it would be particularly useful in coordinating operations with army branches in the nearby suburbs—Niagara Falls, Tonawanda, Watertown, Dunkirk and such. Emergency calls to those offices might be handled more efficiently by a Buffalo volunteer if one were in the vicinity, and vice versa. Those branches with supply shortages could broadcast for help and troubleshooter volunteers could call on portable units for additional assignments without first searching out a telephone and waiting indefinitely for an open line.

The major obstacle to using the ham radio that night was that Salvation Army staffer Bob Harvey of North Buffalo, the only one licensed to operate the facility, would not be able to reach headquarters until morning. Still, that would be soon enough to put the equipment into service, everyone decided, for, as the night progressed, the calls would slacken.

But sometime between midnight and the following dawn, while refugees from the storm slept on the floor and others continued making sandwiches and coffee in the Golden Age Club wing, looters broke into the darkened rooms of the adjoining building and stole the ham-radio equipment.

Since early Friday afternoon, Red Cross personnel on Delaware Avenue had been busily preparing for the storm. Eight shelters were opened throughout Erie County, and headquarters workers set about making sandwiches and coffee.

By two o'clock, calls had gone out to snowmobile clubs all over the area, and by evening, scores of volunteers were delivering food to the temporary shelters, blood to some hospitals that had run low, and drugs—particularly insulin—to those stranded at home.

*

Firefighters descended upon Whitney Place in strings from every direction. They hitched rides to the neighborhood on passing snowmobiles and four-wheel drives, came in National Guard trucks, rode with the plows. Blocks from the fire, where the congestion began and the red light of an impotent fire truck sent churning blades of red across the snow, the men continued on foot. Like a phantom army they appeared out of the snow and stinging smoke, helping to tug hoses along the way, push equipment closer to hydrants, wrestle with couplings and nozzles.

The army of firefighters and neighbors had dragged about two dozen lines to the fire, and the intersection of Whitney and Virginia resembled a giant bowl of spaghetti. Surrounding the fire, hoses sprayed the flames continuously—none could be shut off or the water in them would freeze immediately. The water settled like a mist on the men and froze. With reversing winds, those whose faces were fire-scorched now shivered, and those who had ached with the cold now felt the sting of heat. None were seriously burned but many were frostbitten.

There was no hero to be singled out that night on Whitney Place, for each company was on its own for the most part, each man fighting his own often uncoordinated war. And there was no single dramatic moment when the victory was assured. But by eleven o'clock that night, Joe Paul Falzone raised his stinging, bloodshot eyes to gaze again at the store on the corner. The house next to it had burned to the ground, and the rear of the one on Virginia still smoldered. Even then, a board lay across the store's roof still burning. But the firemen were training hoses on it, and the snow itself was helping to extinguish it.

He did not run to the Ultima Cupa, where his family had gathered to keep warm—he had no energy for that. And when he opened the door, he spoke with finality, as though they were the last words he would utter: "It's not gonna burn, Dad—the store's not gonna burn."

That night, a black family, the Thomases, who lived five doors from what was once the finest house on Whitney Place, invited all five Falzones, their gerbils and their dog to stay with them. The hosts slept on the floor.

*

During the night, reports of the stranded accumulated in ever-growing piles on the desk of Bill Strobele, the police dispatcher. Seventeen hundred day-shift workers and twelve passersby were marooned at Bell Aerosystems in Wheatfield; 2,500 at the Harrison Radiator Company in Lockport; 100 elementary-school students in the Royalton-Hartland Central School in Middleport. Authorities were estimating that at least 13,000 people had been stranded in downtown Buffalo alone, and again that many throughout the entire storm area.

What troubled Strobele most, though, was the fear that many hundreds, perhaps thousands, were still sitting in their cars on the thruways, Skyway and Fuhrmann Boulevard. Even if they'd started out with full tanks, they'd be running out of gas soon. Some would then abandon their cars to seek shelter; they could survive in a windchill factor of minus 50 degrees no more than a few minutes. Remaining in their cars, protected from the wind, they could hope for several hours more. But by morning or soon after there would be little hope.

Strobele had already heard of several rescues. A snowmobile squad from Boston, New York, had found several truckers on the thruway where they'd been marooned since the Wednesday night–Thursday morning squall. Others patrolled the Skyway and the expressway north toward Niagara Falls, discovering dozens of people shivering or unconscious in their vehicles. In another case, a man had telephoned the Wyandotte Cement Company on Fuhrmann Boulevard to say he'd just received a message over his citizen's band radio from a driver who'd been stranded all day at an intersection near the plant. Using a snowmobile and a tractor, Wyandotte employees drove across the towering snowbanks to the intersection to discover several cars and six cold and frightened people. If these few had been saved, Bill wondered, how many more remained isolated, freezing to death? Certainly hundreds—perhaps thousands.

*

At the airport, Assistant Manager Bob Stone shot down problems as though they were clay pigeons on a skeet-shooting range. His grounds crew had labored for several hours to bring the three planes back from the runway to the terminal. The signal men had guided the pilots through radio communication, for they had been unable to see from their cockpits the men on the ground below. Inch by inch, one at a time, they had led the planes back to the terminal.

That night the runways remained closed. With zero visibility, no airline would attempt to land or take off. But Stone issued a standing order: At the first break in visibility, put every piece of equipment to work cleaning up again.

Stone's most pressing problem, once the planes had returned to the terminal, was the hundreds of people swarming through the buildings. By midevening, the airport crawled with more people than Stone had ever seen there, hundreds who had arrived by plane before the blizzard struck, others who had come to the airport that morning with families and friends to take outgoing flights. Scores of motorists, snowbound on busy Genesee Street, had also found their way to the terminal.

Stone wasn't worried about feeding them all—the airport restaurant had plenty of food, and the airlines had already provided tables of free pastry and coffee from the cancelled flights. The overriding need was for sitting and sleeping facilities, at least for the women and children.

It was a soft-spoken, fifty-five-year-old airport janitor, Stanley Kowalewski, who performed the miracle Stone needed. Neither the blizzard's premature arrival nor its violence had come as a surprise to Stanley, for early that morning a charming young stewardess from a flight out of Chicago had already told him, "Christ, we just went through a *hell* of a storm, and it's gonna kick the *shit* out of Buffalo!"

His assignment that morning—to clean the airport sidewalks with a snowblower—seemed absurd in light of the impending blizzard, but he did his job that day, as he had for decades, with good-natured patience. In fact, throughout the day, although he could see only a few feet ahead, he periodically returned to the chore he was given—cleaning the sidewalks with the snowblower.

At about eight o'clock that evening, when Stanley thought it was time that the youngsters be put to bed, he went to the basement of the East Terminal, found a heavy-duty dolly and rolled it back into the long-neglected storage area. There he found the hundreds of old cots Civil Defense had stockpiled years earlier. A few minutes later, he unloaded them on the terminal's second floor. A few volunteers helped with the second load, then scores pitched in, and soon hundreds of cots filled the lounge areas. Other cots were loaded on the airport's fire-fighting equipment and taken to the West Terminal.

Stanley Kowalewski himself carried four of the cots to his friends in the Weather Bureau offices, setting up one of his own in a quiet corner. While he was there Ed Reich, the assistant forecaster, answered a continuing clamor of phones, many from news offices. One call was from Radio Warsaw, another from a Texas radio station, another from Honolulu. Pilots walked in and out requesting forecasts, and one staffer kept saying, "What you see is what you get."

Many veteran airport personnel visited the forecast room, some requesting the latest weather predictions, others to escape the crowds for a short while and relax among friends. Ben Kolker and the day shift continued working, for the night staff had been unable to reach the airport. To the queries of pilots and maintenance men alike, Ben and his colleagues offered the same response: After more than ten hours of the worst blizzard in the city's history, it seemed to be as fierce as ever. Even if the storm's frenzy abated for a time, all the indications pointed to continual snow for the next several days.

*

In downtown Buffalo, the telephone company was deep in unprecedented challenges. Since late that morning, when Larry Mark had peered from the windows of the M&T Building to see a tidal wave of snow rolling across the city, pandemonium seemed to break loose. Although most businesses had closed early, the city's residents placed a record 1,024,310 direct-dial, long-distance calls, almost twice the usual number for a weekday. The 152,800 operator-assisted calls, twice the usual load, set a record of its own. And local calls approached ten million, more than 75 percent above normal.

As the work load grew, so did the realization that many of the approximately 120 operators scheduled for the evening shift would not be reporting. Such a shortage was unthinkable—in fact, the company would need at least 60 more operators than usual to handle the overwhelming demand. Like generals preparing a major defense, telephone company supervisors set about marshaling their depleted forces for the assault that would peak by early evening. They called operators living nearby and pleaded with them to come in if possible; some walked to the operations building on Franklin Street, across from Police Headquarters. Others hitchhiked, hailing a passing emergency vehicle on its way downtown. The company dispatched its emergency van and some of its heavy-duty line vehicles to pick operators up at their homes and ferry them to Franklin Street.

Still, there were not enough operators. Finally the call went out to every worker in the Franklin Street building, company's headquarters in the M&T Building, and other staff locations around the city. Anyone on the staff—clerical, supervisory, or executive—with any operator experience at all was asked to report to Franklin Street and work overnight as an operator.

Soon, an army of volunteers plunged through the blizzard's most violent winds along the course Bill Strobele had followed less than an hour earlier, and that night 185 people manned the switchboards, while others formed a relief crew.

By midevening, there remained one significant problem: how to feed the nearly one thousand people who, stranded in the building, would spend the night there. Shortly after three that afternoon, the crew who managed the Franklin Street building's cafeteria franchise began locking up the facilities and leaving. Larry Evola, head of operator services, cornered the manager and told him that the cafeteria would be essential that night, since a great many people would be stranded, but when Evola returned later, he found the gates to the cafeteria area chained and locked, the lights out and the crew gone.

Evola immediately called the president of the company holding the cafeteria franchise, who agreed to leave his home and personally open the facilities. Two hours passed and no one arrived.

Once again, Evola called the executive, this time with the warning that if the lock wasn't opened in half an hour, he'd break it. He waited another hour, then ordered a maintenance man to bring the wire cutters.

A few minutes later, a crew also broke the locks from two of the refrigerators in the storage room, and that night, with the phone company employees doing the cooking—and keeping impeccable records of the food used—about a thousand people ate well.

15

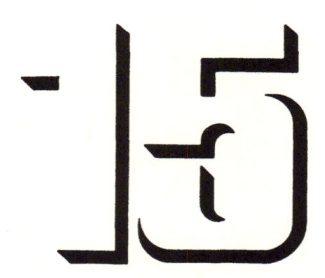

Jeff Hensey, trudging the open expanse of Seneca Street with Clare, lifted his face to the stinging snow. The storm—or perhaps the liquor—had filled him with a sense of intense aliveness. Here, amid the icy relics of a ruined world, people were no doubt freezing to death. Looters stalked the shadows, unintimidated by the storm's violence. Artifices were falling away, and life was, for this one moment, singularly uncomplex: There existed only one enemy, the blizzard; one commitment, survival. And that simplicity enlarged life, it seemed to Jeff, giving some profound significance to each act and word. Here on this lonely stretch of street with Clare, he stumbled, half-drunk, into history. Someday the encyclopedias would have something to say about this place and night. People would write books about it, perhaps make a movie, and although no one would single out Jeff Hensey's story, he would still be among the thousands whose story it would be. He would tell his grandchildren and maybe his great-grandchildren of January 28, 1977. He would tell them the story—but not the whole story, of course.

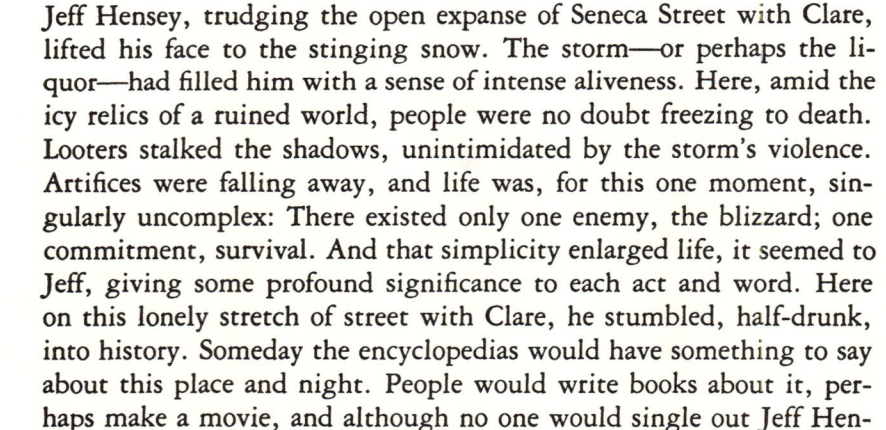

Stopping beneath a street light, he pulled Clare to him. Taking the scarf from his mouth, he pushed hers aside, too. The snow gathered and melted at the point where their lips touched.

He wanted to make love to her right there in the snow—the idea was all the more compelling because it was so absurd. The way the drifts were blowing, they'd be buried alive, and he'd end up with frostbitten loins. He decided to find a hallway instead.

They found many refuges that night. Once, when the wind

overwhelmed them, they climbed into an abandoned bus, huddled together, opened buttons and zippers, fondling each other into a pure red glow of heat, teasing the fire. From there, they stopped at every bar along the way, knocked on a lighted window to beg coffee from a stranger. Hour after hour they continued, never more than a few blocks at a time, lingering for a while at the firehouse at Seneca and Swann, stumbling past Michigan and Myrtle, where the live wire pulsed and contorted, shooting a brilliant, rhythmic spray of white-hot sparks into the air.

From that point they traveled in darkness, for even the streetlights had failed. Shortly after midnight they passed Chef's Restaurant.

"Ain't we gonna stop?" the girl asked.

"I know a better place—besides, we just stopped in that hallway back there. You wearing out on me?"

"Fat chance you'll wear *me* out!" she laughed.

Earlier, fresh from McTrevor's, they'd thrown snowballs into the wind to have them hurled back in their own faces, leaped from car roof to car roof, even rolled together once in the snow. But soon they were wet and weary, and they'd quickly settled into the chore of their journey. Now, Jeff felt renewed vigor, almost joy, which he attributed to intoxication and a half-frozen brain. He took the girl's hand, and with the wind at his back, led her in a stumbling plunge along Seneca Street past the cars standing like monstrous tombstones in a snow-covered graveyard, past the madcap pattern of drifts and hollows that appeared suddenly like abandoned foxholes. Death everywhere, and for him and the girl, nothing but the desolation, no tomorrow, no judges, juries, clients, only now, and the ecstatic heat glowing inside him.

At a street where earlier Bill Strobele had watched a police officer attempt to clear three cars and a dump truck from the cluttered intersection, Jeff and the girl turned left to a tavern.

About a dozen men sat at the bar, their faces ruddy in the flickering light of the candles that lined the counter and reflected in the liquor bottles and glasses. The room smelled of stale beer and candles. It was cold, heated by a pot-bellied stove in an open room adjoining the bar. The men wore coats and spoke softly among themselves as the two travelers stepped inside. Then, with exclamations of astonishment, they led Jeff and Clare to the bar, helped remove their ice-stiffened scarves and hats and offered them drinks.

"Two scotch and sodas—and forget the *ice*," said Jeff.

Someone brought empty chairs from the far end of the bar and squeezed them into the semicircle around the beer tap and bartender, and persuaded Jeff to describe the storm's ferocity. He did so cheerfully, with melodrama and flair, to the men's delight. Later, he tried to tell them what would make the night unforgettable for him, what would bring it back when, gray and aged, he spent his days and evenings rocking on the porch and watching the traffic pass. It would not be the *events* of this night but its brutal honesty. The *reality* of it made him feel abundantly alive. No one understood him, and he finally decided he was making no sense.

"Shit—give everybody another drink," he said.

He dropped a twenty-dollar bill on the counter and led the girl by the hand to the open room with the pot-bellied stove. Jeff found two chairs and moved them near the stove. Instead of sitting beside him, Clare sat on his lap, shivering and holding him tightly, her cold nose pressed against his throat. He caressed her hair and growled in her ear, rocking to rhythm with the music playing in his head. He slipped his hand under her skirt. Soon she stopped shivering, and her body grew warm in his hands.

He thought he'd never been so drunk before. The room seemed made of gelatin, with walls and floors undulating. He pulled at her panties, and with her help they slid down to her knees. He controlled her then, making her groan, even beg in whispers and kisses, for his touching.

Later, while her panties lay on the floor near the pot-bellied stove, he carried her to the darkest corner of the room. She unbuckled his belt, unzipped his trousers, pulled them down and laughed when she saw the long johns. He laughed, too, and then some of the men at the bar laughed. For a moment he fumbled in vain efforts to find the small opening in the underwear. Then, cursing, stumbling, he pulled the long johns off and threw them against the wall.

There was applause from the other room.

It had better be the end of the world, he thought, lifting her legs to his shoulders, kissing her thighs. He'd not have done this in a private motel room a day ago, wouldn't even have talked like this to a girl. Feelings he'd once have denied were even possible now overwhelmed him—and he felt no guilt, only self-satisfaction that he could make a woman feel this way, that the fire could burn so hot. He half lowered himself, half fell upon her, for his body felt like soggy dough and he had little control over it. But she helped him, guided him, and there came an instant when his whole mind filled with the vision of that thrashing electric wire on Myrtle Street, defying with the fury of its gushing sparks all the anger of the wind, the deadly cold, melting even the ice with its heat.

*

At about that time, Rose Ann Wagner hung up the telephone at Emil's Inn. She'd just spoken with her husband for the seventh time that night, assuring him once again that everything continued to be fine and that the eighteen men trapped at the bar, although mostly drunk, were behaving themselves in exemplary fashion. Some had already fallen asleep on the floor, while others continued to argue about which was the very worst blizzard in the nation's history. The younger men had insisted it was the storm of '62, and some had argued for one in the thirties, but the gray-haired men had laughed with scorn. There had been only one really great blizzard, they'd confided, so furious that even today the history books refer to it as the Great Blizzard: the storm of March 11–13, 1888.

While the snoring and talk intermingled with the occasional clanking of glasses, Rose Ann and her mother climbed the stairs to the second floor.

"Now get some sleep," her mother yelled, "and keep your hands off the booze!" To cheers, the women made their way to their rooms. It had been a long, wearying day, but a delightfully exciting one, thought Rose Ann Wagner, and she soon fell into a deep, contented sleep.

*

For more than two hours, the two-vehicle caravan from the Delaware Park Labor Center had been snaking south on Main Street, Mark DuMond at the wheel of the giant tow truck, Al Hoffman at his side, and Angelo Pintabowa in the antiquated bus behind him. Progress had been frustratingly slow, but the trio had confronted few serious challenges, for the multitude of abandoned vehicles cluttering Main Street were staggered among the road's four lanes to allow tortured passage. During the journey, even the wind offered occasional assistance, shifting to blow open a small path that had been buried moments earlier under tons of snow.

The trip became a trial in monotony measured in streetlights that appeared with the regularity of markings on a ruler, each illuminating a landscape so similar to the previous one that they could well have been duplicates of a single scene.

Mark had seen not a single pedestrian along the route, but as he approached the downtown area, headlights occasionally appeared through the snow and he would come upon another vehicle. In the course of an hour, he passed an ambulance, a telephone company truck and two snowmobiles.

His plan was to go south to Summer Street, then west toward the lake, finally connecting with Niagara and turning south again for the few blocks to the TOPS and Superduper Markets, where, if everyone else had done his job, literally hundreds of boxes of food would be packed and crews would be standing by to load them. But the farther south he drove, the heavier became the snow accumulation, and before he was half a block along Summer, Mark knew that the previous two hours of unrelieved tension would prove the easy part of the trip.

Early that morning of the twenty-ninth, while Bill Strobele was dispatching the remnants of his Police Department to desperate callers, while Jeff Hensey and the girl were embracing and Rose Ann Wagner was sleeping soundly, Angelo Pintabowa was shivering at the wheel of a heaterless bus and Mark DuMond was pushing and towing the first car from his path.

With the road clear, Mark plunged through two blocks of snowdrifts before Angelo's plaintive voice reached him over the citizen's band: He was no longer following DuMond but had lost traction in the snow. DuMond backed up, and while Pintabowa sat with teeth chattering and hands and feet growing increasingly painful, Al Hoffman connected a chain from the truck to the bus bumper.

"Something's burning out there," Al said when he got back into the truck.

The tow truck easily pulled the bus from the gripping snow and, except for one tight squeeze in which the rear bumper of the bus scraped a protruding car, the two vehicles reached Niagara Street without incident. From there Mark had at first anticipated an easy conclusion to the assignment, for, turning south on Niagara, he would cross only three streets—Jersey, Pennsylvania and Hudson—to reach the two supermarkets just before Maryland. Thereafter, continuing on Niagara a few more blocks, he'd come upon City Hall. Since Niagara was a major four-lane road, it would certainly be open.

Seven blocks away, however, the mouth of the Niagara River had lain frozen and snow-covered from bank to bank even longer than the rest of the lake. Into this narrowing funnel at Lake Erie's northeastern tip, the wind had raced with increasing fury to hurl its greatest assault against Niagara Falls and Grand Island to the north, Fort Erie in Canada, and the nearby Buffalo shore—particularly Niagara Street north of City Hall. Mark drove a single block south, to

Jersey Street, and then even the tow truck could go no farther. Dozens of stalled trucks, cars and buses combined with monstrous snowdrifts and blinding snow to make even foot travel for the remaining two and a half blocks out of the question.

Still, there was no place to turn the bus around. The alternative—an almost impossible one—was for Angelo to back the bus to the Porter Street intersection, through the snow that had blown and fallen behind it, without the aid of the tow truck in breaking a path, and in spite of the fact that the bus had little weight over the rear tires. What's more, with the snow driving so hard, Angelo couldn't even *see* the rear of the bus.

With Al and Mark shouting directions, Angelo, with snow blowing into his face through the open window, slowly, tediously, inched the bus back toward the intersection. Twice it bogged down in snowbanks and Mark towed it forward again. Finally it reached Porter.

Even there, the bus couldn't be turned around, but Mark managed to get the truck behind it to at least break the snow with the heavy tires. Its flashing lights served as a dimly blinking beacon to guide Angelo.

An hour later, they had backed the bus six blocks. At Richmond Street, Angelo followed the tow truck south again along Allen to Maryland, one block south of the supermarkets, and headed back toward Niagara. Now the smell of smoke was stronger than ever. Held close to the ground by an impenetrable blanket of cold air, it appeared as a massive fog, battling to dominate the driving snow. The three were almost to Whitney Place, a block north of Virginia, when, through the dense sky, they first recognized the glow of flames. Then they came upon a fire-department car and truck blocking the street. Mark found the car empty, but two firemen were slumped in the seat of the truck, the engine running. He feared they'd been overcome by exhaust fumes, but they were only sleeping.

"Fire's under control," one of them said. "Hell of a night. We're wrecked. So's the equipment. Half an hour more and the engine in this thing's finished." The truck would run out of gasoline by then, he explained, and without antifreeze in the engine the water would freeze and crack the block.

"So go back to the firehouse."

"Yeah—we're frozen solid in the runoff."

"Well, I gotta get ya outta my way," said Mark, adding dryly, "Mayor's orders."

103

A few minutes later, Al Hoffman had attached the tow-truck lift to the fire vehicle and Mark wrenched it free from the ice. He towed it far enough to the side so that Al could get the bus past, lowered it, then pushed the car aside. From that point, they were only two blocks from Niagara. Yet, Mark had to tow or push four more cars out of his path in that short distance.

Again on Niagara, the road was impossibly jammed, but the TOPS Market was only two buildings from the intersection on the right, and the Superduper not much farther away on the other side of the street. Mark drove the tow truck onto the sidewalk, then moved back and forth to pack an adequate path for the bus. After Angelo negotiated the turn, Al Hoffman hooked the chain to the bus and the caravan, winding between streetlights and fire hydrants, plate-glass windows and snowbanks, proceeded along the sidewalk to TOPS Market.

More than five hours had elapsed since the three had left the Delaware Park Labor Center.

*

Although Street Sanitation Commissioner James Lindner had called his crews back soon after the blizzard struck, not all his men had returned. Forty-three-year-old Bill Kennedy had been following the plows along Fuhrmann Boulevard in his autocar diesel with a salt spreader Friday morning when the storm struck. Like thousands of others, Kennedy expected no more than a brief squall, and waited patiently for improved visibility. Nine o'clock that night, he still waited.

By then, Bill Kennedy had no hope of driving back to the Broadway Garage, for the autocar had been snowbound for several hours. Using the vehicle's two-way radio, he'd kept in continuous communication with the Broadway Garage, and Lindner had sent several men to rescue him. But Kennedy could not give his exact location, and with roads impassable and visibility virtually zero, finding the autocar amounted to a virtually impossible task.

Instead, the men searching for Kennedy plowed their way along part of the Skyway, where they discovered fourteen stranded motorists. Commandeering a small schoolbus, they plowed a path from the Skyway to the Hotel Statler and took the people there.

Long after midnight, Bill Kennedy reported that he'd run out of fuel. At Lindner's request, volunteers on snowmobiles swarmed into the area. Another hour passed. Then someone reported what appeared to be a flashing yellow light. It could have been from Kennedy's autocar, but it was coming from an area inaccessible to ordinary vehicles, and the caller was unable to investigate further. Immediately, snowmobiles converged on the area, some skimming over the rooftops of buried cars.

It was almost 2 A M when Bill Kennedy radioed in a weary, almost lifeless voice that his rescuers had found him. At the Broadway Garage, his friends, toughened by years of rugged service in the streets, celebrated the good news with hugs and tears.

16

A few minutes after 2 A.M., Jeff and Clare reached Chef's Restaurant The air was thick with cigarette smoke, and people seemed to be everywhere—sleeping on the floor and tables, conversing quietly in huddled groups. In the dim candlelight of the nearest dining room, Jeff saw what appeared the remains of a large cake. Recognizing Lou Billittier, the owner, he nodded toward the table.

"Is that fit for human consumption?" he asked.

"Since when're you raising your standards?" quipped Billittier. "The lady hungry?"

"Well, we didn't drop in to see your pretty face.

"Help yourself. My kid's eighteenth birthday today. We kinda threw that together, had a little party. That's all there is—cupboard's bare. Christ, even the coffeemaker's out. No damn electricity."

"I know."

"We're boiling the beans on the gas stove!"

At the table with Billittier sat several policemen: Fred Clark, Carl Reese, Norman Wojtkowiak and Joseph Ramsford. Both Clark and Reese officially worked out of police headquarters on Franklin Street, but had been snowbound at the restaurant for several hours.

"At least it's warm in here," someone said. "You got gas heat?"

"The heat's out," said Billittier, "but why worry? There's enough hot air at this table to keep the place warm all winter Besides, the oven's going full blast."

Lou Billittier's deadpan manner was intended to alleviate the anxiety he'd seen in some of those stranded in the restaurant. In fact, however, Lou himself felt increasing concern. For one thing, the temperature had already dropped noticeably. And he hadn't been kidding when he told Jeff the cupboard was bare.

And the storm showed no signs of abating.

Lou glanced toward a dark corner of the main dining room where a man who had been on his way home from the hospital after getting a diagnosis of terminal cancer slept on the floor beside his wife, a coat draped over him. In the morning, Lou would pull some strings, get him a room at the Statler. He knew a lawyer with an office there. Something could be worked out. In another part of the room, a twenty-three-year-old woman rested. Said her name was Phyllis Parkhurst, pregnant and diabetic, said she needed insulin. Officer Wojtkowiak had already used his radio to request the drug from Emergency Hospital, half a mile away. They'd try to deliver it. Food. He had a friend who ran a vending-machine company. Maybe he'd have some doughnuts or something. Lou would call him in the morning.

Right here: About 220 people, sleeping fitfully, smoking, whispering among themselves, pacing where they found space, all counting on Lou Billittier. The party was coming to an end. The storm had been an inconvenience, then an adventure, an excuse for celebration. Now it had become possible that people by the hundreds would freeze to death. One by one, this cross section of society that had sought shelter here—presidents and vice-presidents of major corporations, housewives, laborers, children and aged—were coming to recognize the danger. And they all looked to Lou.

At about 2:30 A.M., a few people decided to go to the Puerto Rican Center on Swann Street. When they refused to be dissuaded, officer Fred Clark offered to guide them.

They stepped from the restaurant into a furious gust of wind. As Officer Clark started up the snowbank at the curb, the wind shifted, hurling him back and off balance. He fell on his right leg, fracturing it.

Carl Reese and other officers carried him inside and placed him on a table, splinted the leg and wrapped him in blankets. Billittier called Emergency Hospital again for an ambulance.

Two and a half hours later, at five A.M., neither an ambulance nor Phyllis Parkhurst's insulin had arrived, and Officer Carl Reese,

107

who hadn't been feeling well himself, went to talk to her. Without insulin, she would probably go into a diabetic coma at about 6:30, she explained.

Officer Reese waited another hour. When the ambulance still hadn't arrived at six A.M., he and Officer Norman Wojtkowiak set out on foot for Emergency Hospital, half a mile north of Chef's on Eagle and Pine streets.

With the dawn, visibility had improved slightly, but the temperature still hovered around 7 degrees below zero with a windchill factor of minus 60. To breathe, the officers walked backwards into the wind. Only by shouting could they communicate. More than once they ducked into a hallway to rest and grow warm.

On the way back to the restaurant, Officer Reese stumbled and slumped against a building.

"Boy, I'm out of shape," he yelled to Wojtkowiak. "Can't breath—and I got indigestion in the bargain." Finally, they continued, and reached the restaurant to give the medication to an anxious and grateful Mrs. Parkhurst at about 6:45.

Soon after, Jeff and the girl left. Standing on the snowbank where officer Clark had fallen, Jeff could hear the distant rumble of heavy equipment digging toward the downed line on Myrtle Avenue. Except for that, the only sounds were of the wind and snow.

He held Clare tightly. She would be going north now, he west. They'd spent the Great Blizzard together, stepped into history in each other's arms, and he didn't even know her address. And this was the end of it, as though it had meant nothing.

"Look, maybe . . ."

She shook her head violently, and seemed to force a smile.

"It's been nice," she told him, and kissed him quickly. "See ya."

He watched her stumble through the snow, into the street, weaving her way between the cars. The snow stung his eyes. He squinted, and when he looked for her again there was only the whiteness.

He turned and walked east, the wind at his back.

*

Between 8 A.M., and midnight Friday, the Niagara Mohawk Utility Company had received 3,283 phone calls, almost three times the usual, many to report power failures, a few either comic or absurd:

"I'm moving Monday no matter what's with the weather," one caller announced, "so don't forget to change my electricity over."

Another insisted on speaking to Bill Vogel, head of the complaint department, personally: "The streetlight in front of my house ain't working, and I want it fixed now!"

Vogel spent most of Friday fielding complaints of power outages, and by six o'clock that evening he had made a curious discovery—according to his figures, 89 percent of those without power needed it restored immediately because they had newborn babies and grandmothers living with them.

Actually, most power failures were restored within twenty minutes to an hour and a half, and the company had enough surplus workers and equipment available to help others fight the storm. Niagara Mohawk loaned six four-wheel drive vehicles to Jefferson County, and plowed open the central access roads to the county's major disaster center. Using its heavy equipment, company workers shuttled stranded motorists to shelters and transported hospital personnel to work.

The Salvation Army had called Bud Kitson at the power company headquarters in center city seeking transportation for two children who had been abandoned in the snow. Bud got janitors Nick Cordova and John Nowak to drive in Nick's jeep to the Salvation Army headquarters, pick up the children and deliver them to a foster home fifteen miles away. Other company workers delivered food, drugs, groceries and similar necessities.

When Bill Strobele called Niagara Mohawk to report the downed line on Myrtle Avenue, the company was already "knee-deep in alligators," as troubleshooter Mert Wagner put it. The most pressing problem: Cars and snow had effectively blockaded the vital Dewey Avenue Service Center, near Main Street, three miles north of center city.

"When's the city gonna plow us out?" John Boyd, supervisor of building construction, asked Strobele.

"You want me to name the month, or just the year?"

"Look, we gotta get outta here if you want that line fixed. We can plow the road ourselves—but we gotta tow the cars out first, and we're not touching 'em till somebody down there takes the responsibility."

"So move 'em already," said Strobele.

While the company was clearing Dewey Avenue, a line super-

109

visor in south Buffalo started north toward Myrtle to appraise the damage there. He got as far as Ohio and Childs streets on the bank of the Buffalo River, a few blocks from the Skyway and Fuhrmann Boulevard, before the snow trapped his vehicle. From there, he continued on foot to the company's station 17, where he phoned the trouble officer to explain his predicament.

By then, another worker, Louis LaPlaca, had reached station 41, which housed the breaker, cutting electricity to three of the six wires on the pole, including the fallen one.

At about the time Officer Clark broke his leg and Rose Ann Wagner decided to go to bed, another Niagara Mohawk troubleshooter, Don Clark, set out from the Dewey Avenue Center to the Myrtle Avenue break in a peculiar-looking four-wheel drive vehicle called a power wagon. Its most unusual features were great balloon tires designed to break a path through snow and sand so that the bucket truck could follow. Clark drove the truck south on Main, under radio guidance from Strobele. He and the other dispatchers at police headquarters, relying on field reports from scores of people, had drawn a map of the city on which was indicated the streets remaining open and those which were impassable. Now, relying on that map, Strobele guided Clark through an intricate maze toward the break.

At the same time, Strobele kept in touch with the Seneca Street Garage. Somehow the police officers had climbed to the top of the heavy garage door, chipped and melted the ice and finally, with an effort that astonished even themselves, raised the door manually. Now they were asking Strobele for directions.

"Your first job's just about outside your door," he told them. "Get that junk outta the intersection there. Get up to the next block, Myrtle, left. Clear it out there straight down to Michigan. You gotta get Michigan opened north—at least a couple blocks north. The electric company's coming down there, and it's jammed curb to curb."

Long before Don Clark reached the neighborhood of the downed wire, the power wagon began faltering. Climbing up and through the snow put such a strain on the engine that it stalled repeatedly, and continual restarting had drained the battery until finally it died.

They'd need another battery, and bringing it from the Dewey Avenue Center might take hours. Already the break had cut power to some neighborhoods for more than twelve hours. Many were no doubt freezing. Others, with electric stoves, might not have had a warm meal or a hot cup of coffee since Friday noon, if then.

Don brushed the snow from the hood of the nearest car. While other crewmen removed the battery and installed it in the power wagon, Don scribbled a note explaining where the battery had gone and why. Half an hour later the great balloon tires began chugging forward again.

Still two blocks from Myrtle on Michigan, Don came upon an impassable accumulation of abandoned vehicles. Above the wind he could hear the equipment from the Seneca Street Garage, the clanking of metal on metal, the scraping of pavement. But it was already 6:30 A.M., growing light, and there was no time to wait. He left the power wagon and trudged the remaining distance through the storm.

Coming upon the pole with the dead wire dangling beside it, he discovered with relief that it was no major problem, only a simple break resulting no doubt from a particularly violent blast of wind. It would be easy enough to fix, but he'd need the bucket and the equipment in the truck. Until the road was cleared, he could only wait and watch.

For three hours the big machines tore into the snowbanks. Tow trucks yanked cars by the dozens to the cleared areas. A bulldozer hurled the snow from the road like a giant fist, then stomped it into rock hardness so that the wind couldn't sweep it up again.

Long before Myrtle Avenue was cleared, Buffalo awakened.

17

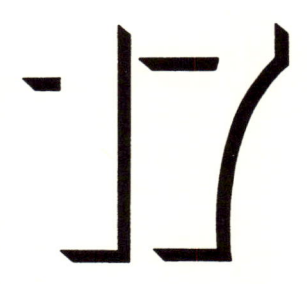

Dawn came to a lifeless city. In the gray morning, no traffic moved along the downtown stretch of major streets. Delaware, Main, Genesee, Court, Niagara—every avenue leading to Niagara Square and City Hall was still. Lafayette Square was empty. Those who peered from the windows of Hengerer's Department Store felt a sense of doom, as though some Vesuvius had buried the city under a cold white ash.

At about 7 A M, the sound of two rumbling engines and the intermittent tearing of metal reached Niagara Square. Mark DuMond's tow truck broke out of Niagara Street to attack a car obstructing the circle there. He pushed another car, and still another out of his path before plunging along the sidewalk to the door of City Hall. A moment later, Angelo Pintabowa maneuvered the bus to the space Mark had cleared in front of the building. Behind Pintabowa, cartons of food reached higher than the windows. Four hundred loaves of bread cluttered the seats. Cases rested against the back of Angelo's head, jammed the aisle beside him, cluttered the steps. Only after a dozen boxes were removed could he leave the bus.

"Great job, boys, great job," said Bob Rung, City Hall's Director of General Services. He urged Angelo, who was trembling and pale with the cold and the night's unrelieved tension, to go inside and have a cup of coffee, but then to hurry back to the bus—he would be needed for other emergencies.

Angelo handed Rung the keys. "There," he said. "It's parked,

112

and as far as I'm concerned, there it stays. You don't like it, fire me."

He took a couple of bags of groceries from the bus, tossed them into the tow truck and climbed in next to Al Hoffman.

"Home, James," he told Mark, and they careened around the circle toward Delaware Avenue.

At that hour, Mayor Stanley Makowski was meeting again with his staff. The Buffalo *Courier-Express* had failed to publish that morning for the first time in 143 years and the *Evening News* wouldn't come out for several hours yet, but police, fire and other emergency reports had already established some idea of the storm's impact: thirteen thousand stranded, several dead, frozen in the snow or in their cars, the entire city shut down and business losses amounting to more than a million dollars a day.

James Lindner told the mayor that he'd already sent his crews back on the streets, for visibility had improved slightly. Even so, the work would still demand great caution—already that morning two huge New York Department of Transportation plows clearing a rural highway had bogged down side by side in a snow-covered ditch and wouldn't be removed for days.

His crews, said Lindner, were performing incredibly well. It was an impossible job, yet most of the men had tapped some inner energy source—call it guts, or stubbornness—and they were going on and on, re-opening the same roads every few hours. Now, with the National Guard's help, they were hoping to clear access to some of the hospitals, where even four-wheel drives were reporting some difficulty.

But it was crazy to think that the city's equipment, limping and broken, was any match for this storm, Lindner said. The businessmen were screaming about losing money because nobody could get downtown to shop. Well, they'd go right on losing money till spring if they were waiting for the Streets Department to get rid of the snow. The time to have worried about snow removal was when requests for more and newer equipment were tabled, when an emergency snow-removal plan involving private contractors was set aside.

Now, said Lindner, it was up to the governor.

Police Commissioner Thomas Blair, too, had unpleasant news for the mayor: The looting was completely out of control. All over the city, looters were breaking into abandoned cars, stealing tape

113

decks and citizen's band radios. Liquor stores were prime targets, with windows smashed and thefts often limited to the easily reached bottles on display.

More than $1,500 in medical supplies had been stolen from a stalled ambulance.

A gang of fifty looters had systematically attacked several blocks of stranded cars and trucks, loading the merchandise on sleds and wagons. Ben's Furniture and Appliances on William Street was stripped clean. A truckload of cigarettes and another of liquor were emptied. One motorist reported that thieves had stolen the only thing of value in his car—his lunch. Scores of homes were ransacked. So were a couple of jewelry stores. The Dan Dee Potato Chip Company lost five hundred dollars' worth of snacks.

"They're like ants," one complainer told a 911 operator. "They take whatever they can on their backs."

Apparently, only one would-be thief had been apprehended at that point. John Prolejko had spent the night in his pharmacy, the Schiller Park Drug Store on Genesee Street, and was awakened early Saturday morning by the sound of splitting wood as someone forced open the front door. He reached for his 12-gauge shotgun and fired. A young man staggered back into the snow, clutching his face, and fled with an accomplice. Police arrested him later and hospitalized him in stable condition.

Commissioner Blair pointed out that private citizens had offered about ten snowmobiles and a few four-wheel drives, and said that, since other agencies were meeting emergency needs, the police department's first priority now was to crack down on looters—and to publicize the department's muscle at least as widely as its immobility had been advertised the night before. The mayor's advisors agreed.

The strain was obvious in Mayor Makowski's face. He'd slept less than an hour, wandering for most of the night through the building's corridors to be sure that everyone was being cared for. He would have liked to turn to someone for advice, but there was no precedent for this monstrous storm. No one had any more experience in this matter than he—and that is what frightened him most. That and the nightmare of hundreds of people dying of heart attacks, and freezing, and suffocating in carbon monoxide fumes. All because he somehow failed.

"Will you pray with me?" he asked, and reporters and advisors bowed their heads.

*

Rose Ann Wagner awakened early. For a moment she lay listening to the sounds of the men below, remembering the holiday spirit of the previous night.

Then she heard the snow brushing the bedroom window, and she realized that the storm continued. Bounding from the bed, she hurried to the window. What she saw could have been a concrete wall or the face of a glacier. An unyielding white wall blocked the glass. Suddenly frightened, Rose Ann stepped back. It was the snow, the incessantly driving snow. The drifts were reaching to the second floor! For a long while she stared into the whiteness. Then she began to cry.

"Might as well be getting 'em breakfast," her mother said from the hallway.

Rose Ann wiped her eyes dry and turned from the window.

*

Don Clark, troubleshooter for Niagara Mohawk, approached the overhead wires. He was eager to get started, for although the storm seemed to suspend time, making of the hours a monotonous span of gray to black, his watch read about 10 A.M. Seven thousand people had been without electricity for about seventeen hours. Still, he raised the bucket with extreme caution. Although the breaker contolling the three lower lines—including the broken one—had been thrown, the three upper wires remained hot, carrying 5,000 volts each, enough to kill a man instantly if he were well grounded. Even with the insulated weather gear, the hot-line mechanic's hat, the insulated boots, even in the partially insulated bucket, a man brushing against one of those wires could suffer heart fibrillation and death. There were other dangers, too. Not long ago a wire had touched the top of a lineman's head and instantly damaged his spine, permanently crippling him.

In weather like this, the snow itself became an effective conductor. Sufficiently dense, it could carry electricity from the wire to the lineman's body.

Next to accidentally hitting one of the live overhead wires, Don Clark's greatest concern was the downed wire that even now flailed in the sixty-mile-an-hour winds. Should that wire make contact with the live ones overhead, it would become instantly energized. In just such a manner, many a lineman working on "dead" wires had been killed.

Clark's job should have been simple—a matter of slipping both ends of the broken wire into a connecting sleeve and crimping them there. But the downed line had burned and frayed until it was several feet too short to make the connection, requiring that the entire length of wire between the two utility poles be removed and replaced.

He raised the bucket to within arm's reach of the maze of wires and locked it in place, then set about rubbering up each of the lines except the broken one. One by one, he slipped a thick, slashed rubber hose around each wire and fastened it with a clothespinlike clip. When a lineman is wet with rain or snow as Clark was, the electricity could easily jump from the wire to the wet suit, through the two pairs of rubber gloves he wore, through the insulated rubber boots to the bucket and kill him. Only the rubber hoses provided dependable protection. What's more, if the lineman should drop the wire he's working on and it hits the rubber hose instead of the live wire, he'd live to laugh about his clumsiness.

Removing the burned-out wire and connecting the new one went quicker than usual in spite of the storm—in fact, because of it. With the wind howling, Clark had realized he'd never have been heard on the ground if he'd yelled down for additional equipment, so he'd brought along in the bucket everything he could conceivably need. That had saved time. And the cold forced him to keep his fingers moving. The two pairs of gloves he wore offered no guarantee against frostbite of the fingers in such weather.

Even before Clark brought the bucket down, the ground crew had already run the new wire to the second pole. But what Clark and the others had feared was now obvious: Several hours more would pass before the bulldozers could remove the cars and mountain of drifts blocking access to the other pole. Clark had two choices: He could allow thousands of people to remain without electricity—and without heat—for those additional hours, or he could climb the pole.

There were good arguments against the climb. Ordinarily, in violent wind, guide wires are strung from a pole and anchored in the ground to offset the lineman's weight and keep the pole from swaying, but now there was nowhere to anchor the wires. The pole would certainly sway and, brittle from the cold, it might snap. If the fall didn't kill Clark, the tangle of live wires could.

He'd use two safety belts, but he'd maintain his footing primarily by the spurs on his boots, each only one and a half inches long. Wood this cold often split under the lineman's weight.

And there was the lack of footing and mobility without the bucket, and a violent, capricious wind.

It was a few minutes after 10 A.M. when Clark snapped the belts around the pole. A cable was attached to the utility belt at his waist, and as he climbed, it reached like an umbilical cord to the ground crew. It would be his only contact with the ground, for, once he reached the wires, they would not be able to hear each other, and even visibility would be virtually zero. He carried with him all his tools. The hoses for rubbering up the wires and the new wire to be attached would come up on the cable.

Again he worked with extreme caution, but faster than ever now, for he was facing the wind and even breathing was difficult. His eyes watered, and the water froze on his lower lids and cheeks. He ignored that, but the growing thickness in his fingers worried him. He dropped a rubber hose, then a couple of clamps. Those were signs of carelessness, or maybe fatigue, warnings that ought not to be ignored.

But there were no accidents. After cutting loose the downed wire, Clark pulled taut the new one, clamped it, tied it in. A few minutes later Lou LaPlaca, who had spent the night alone in tiny cinderblock station 41, engaged the breaker and power surged through the new wire.

It was a job that Don and the crew did day in and day out, a way to make a living, and that was it. But that morning, when Clark stepped down into the snow, one man applauded and another clapped him on the back.

*

While Don Clark was descending the pole, a Buffalo police car from Seneca Street Garage nosed into a newly cleared space in front of Chef's Restaurant. A moment later, Carl Reese and another officer emerged from the building carrying Officer Fred Clark. A moment later the cruiser turned north to Myrtle Avenue, then west past the newly energized wire, then north again on Michigan to Emergency Hopital. Along the way, Officer Reese complained again of indigestion. He thought he might ask the hospital for medication. But when he arrived there, after carrying Officer Clark into the emergency room, he forgot about the discomfort and hurried to answer another emergency. In fact, he continued working until two o'clock that afternoon, three and a half continuous shifts.

*

Richard Rebadow's perfect machine had triumphed. In spite

117

of the continuing wind and snow, Bob Stone and the ground crew at Greater Buffalo International Airport had succeeded in opening the airport that Saturday morning, and at 11:10 a C-130 loaded with cold-weather gear and other National Guard equipment landed during a momentary lull in the storm. It was a feat Rebadow would later be hailed for; now, with rails and highways blocked and access to the city virtually nonexistent, Rebadow's airport, along with one in Niagara Falls, became the city's major lifelines to the outside world.

By 11 A.M., James Lindner had been working for thirty-one hours. At 1:30 the previous afternoon, well before other city officials seemed aware of impending disaster, Lindner had told the mayor, "The streets're gone." Although he'd ordered his men off the roads, he'd kept the entire first shift on duty all night. Then he headed back to the Broad Street Garage with three secretaries from his City Hall office. It was at the garage that all his snow-fighting equipment was stored and serviced and it was from that base, Lindner decided, that he would fight the blizzard.

He put the secretaries to work on the phones immediately. A call was made to the Red Cross to request thirty-five cots. Some workers cleared a space for them on the garage's second floor. Crewmen would spend the night there, ready to go to work at the first break in the storm.

But once visibility improved, there was still an insurmountable problem: Lindner's plows would never get through as long as the streets were cluttered with automobiles. By midnight Friday, an estimated two thousand cars were stalled on Main Street alone. Perhaps eight thousand more cluttered the city streets.

After midnight, he'd sat down with a telephone and a phone book and began calling private towing companies. He was desperate, yet unrelenting in his bargaining:

"It's twenty-five dollars a car, maximum," he'd demanded. "Not even twenty-five dollars and ten cents—I said twenty-five dollars *maximum!*"

By 6 A.M. Saturday, Lindner, acting on his own authority, had thirty private tow trucks on the road, some from as far away as Toronto. Later in the day, there were fifty. And Lindner's plows hit the road.

They worked according to an already established snow removal plan, dividing the city according to councilmanic districts, pinpointing the major roads in each and numbering them according to priority. By attempting to open top priority roads in every district at the same time, they would avoid charges of political favoritism.

That afternoon, he rounded up a few dump trucks and payloaders, and had them cart snow from the city's most congested areas, dumping it into the Niagara River.

"Keep your fingers crossed none of them environmentalists get an idea we're polluting the river," he told an aide, "or before we get dug out we'll be buried again in red tape."

By midafternoon, it was obvious that, in spite of Lindner's efforts, the city would not dig out. The snow had continued falling, and the wind began blowing hard again, throwing new drifts across previously opened roads.

18

When Jeff Hensey reached his brother's house, he phoned his wife. She hadn't slept all night, she said. Weeping, imagining him freezing to death on the Skyway, she'd phoned everyone—the police, the Red Cross, his brother. Finally she'd turned off the radio—the news just frightened her more. Yes, the children were fine; bored, of course, suffering cabin fever, but delighted to see the snow covering all but the last few inches of the huge bay window in the living room. The electricity hadn't failed and the house was warm. She and Nichole had even built a fire in the fireplace.

But why hadn't he phoned?

He told her he'd tried several times, but some of the lines were down and the crowds waiting to use telephones were too long, and once, when he had found a phone available, the lines were jammed and he'd gotten busy signals. He'd spent the night in a bar, he told her, drinking tonic water and lime juice, and finally he'd fallen asleep on a table.

No, there was no way he could get home, probably not for a couple of days yet. He would stay with his brother. Perhaps he would help at Emergency Hospital. Yes, he felt fine. Yes, he loved her—he loved her, very, very much.

Hanging up the phone, he felt overwhelming weariness, and a few minutes later he was asleep on the living room sofa. When he awakened two hours later, his head felt as though it were being

120

beaten with a hammer in perfect rhythm with his heartbeat. While his brother's wife incessantly yelled at the three screaming children, Jeff mixed and drank three cups of instant coffee in succession, and the caffeine, dilating the blood vessels of his brain, brought some measure of relief.

Jeff's request for the keys to the snowmobile introduced the argument he'd anticipated.

"S'ppose we have to get to the store and you got the snowmobile?" said his brother.

"Do you need anything from the store?"

"No, not now—not that I know of. But what if we do?"

"I'll be back, George—I'm not off to Alaska, you know."

"Yeah, but what if you get run over by a goddamn plow? The whole thing could get smashed to hell, and then where'll I be? We'll *never* get to the fucking store."

"That's fine! You're mourning your lousy snowmobile and I'm splattered all over the street!"

Finally Jeff prevailed. Refusing lunch, he hurried out to shovel the snow away from the garage. Soon his brother joined him and they worked silently together.

Late in the afternoon, Jeff gunned the snowmobile and lunged across a snowbank in the driveway. His brother shouted something about taking care of the snowmobile, but before he finished the sentence, Jeff was out of sight. His plan was to go to Emergency Hospital and see if he could be of some use there. Perhaps they needed drugs delivered, or a patient transported from home to the hospital. If not, he'd stop at the Seneca Street Garage, or the firehouse at Seneca and Swann. During the past night, while he and the girl were walking to Chef's, the desire to help had first seized him. The snow had begun falling Wednesday night, and now, with the storm entering the fourth day, it was time to fight back. He had no delusions of grandeur, and, as he skimmed across the snow on his way to the hospital, it seemed to him that this winter might be truly invincible, that mere mortals might be utterly without hope in confronting such savagery. But that wasn't the point at all. The point was that it was time to fight back. Winning or losing was secondary, almost immaterial.

For the thrill of it, he opened the snowmobile up even faster along the cleared section of Michigan. Then, remembering his brother's plea, he slowed the vehicle again. It was crazy, he thought, how content he felt. The house, the cars, the law practice—they'd all made him proud; only this crazy storm had made him content. These days had already changed his life.

*

While Jeff Hensey approached the entrance to Emergency Hospital, a young police officer, Raul Russi, dressed in civilian clothes, hid in the darkened corner of a wig shop in East Buffalo. Russi and his partner, Joe Ransford, had donned two Afro wigs, and seconds later, three young men walked in.

"Hey, man, don't go hogging all the stuff," one of them said. "Come on, let's get some 'a the action."

The three gathered armloads of wigs and accessories and started for the door.

Two more policemen blocked the exit.

"You're busted, boys," Officer Russi announced. It was the eighteenth arrest he and Ransford had made that afternoon, all at the wig shop in precisely the same fashion.

Russi had begun working earlier the previous morning. A plainclothes officer with the streets crime unit, he had been in court as a witness when the storm struck. Afterward, he had walked back to police headquarters, signed out and climbed into his rusting '69 Chevy. He had driven only two blocks, to the approach of the Skyway, before pulling onto the shoulder and parking the car. Visibility was zero, and the wind had already blown the road closed.

Walking back to headquarters, he had tried to borrow another car, but it wouldn't start. For the rest of the day he had done what little he could to help around the station, but by evening, he was bored and frustrated—he wanted to be outside doing something, helping somebody. Finally, at nine o'clock that night, Professor George Adolf of the State University at Buffalo, who owned a four-wheel drive truck, walked into the station and offered to chauffeur some officers around.

Russi's first call was a domestic squabble: A husband had broken his wife's leg and arm. Next, he rescued a couple and their eight children. The snow had blown open their door, and the tiny space heater provided no warmth. The woman had passed out, so Russi and his partner for the evening, Lieutenant James McCann, carried her three blocks to the truck and took her to Columbus Hospital on Niagara Street. For that trip, and the rest of the night, the doors to Adolf's truck had to be tied closed with rope—the locks had frozen.

Traffic blocked access to the hospital for two blocks, so Russi and McCann carried the woman for that distance, too. A reporter for United Press International noted that Russi had no scarf, so he took off his own and gave it to the officer.

An elderly woman who lived on Niagara Street reported that her eighty-year-old husband had died, and Bill Strobele, the dispatcher, radioed the call to "Car 21," as he'd labeled Adolf's truck. An hour later, Russi knocked on Apartment 2C of the Shoreline Apartments. An old woman answered.

"I'm a police officer. Is there a dead person here?" he asked.

"Yes, my husband died. He's been sick for some time. Come in. Would you like a cup of coffee?"

Russi enthusiastically accepted. Later, sitting at the kitchen table, he told her they were living through the worst blizzard in the city's history and there was no way he could remove the body that night.

"Son," she said, "I lived with this man over forty years. A couple more days, dead or alive, is all right with me."

Thus, the night had gone on, from one emergency to another, transporting drugs, food, people. Finally, at about 5:30 A.M., Russi returned to the police station and fell asleep on top of some file cabinets. Awakening three hours later, he was told to go out with Joe Ransford and arrest looters. That's how he'd spent much of Saturday.

He and Ransford had just arrived back at headquarters when Strobele received a call that a tall, muscular man was breaking into rooms at the Statler Hotel, across Niagara Square. The officers jumped into "Car 21" and raced to the hotel, but when they got there, the thief had already fled. Russi and Ransford tracked him to a smaller hotel around the corner, and the desk clerk said that the thief had just gone into the men's washroom. Russi went after him, pulled his revolver and pressed it into the man's back.

"You're under arrest, buddy," he said.

The man turned slowly, towering over the five-foot, eight-inch officer. He stared at Russi, then at the gun.

"I don't wanna know nothing about no guns," he said, pushing the weapon away from his midsection. Then, with more anger, shoving Russi backwards, "Get that gun outta my sight."

Astonished, Russi put the gun away.

The man also didn't want to know nothing about no handcuffs, but following a struggle on the washroom floor, Russi and Ransford managed to subdue and cuff him.

Elsewhere in the city, police were arresting looters wholesale.

By evening, between fifty and sixty had been jailed to await hearings the following day.

*

That afternoon, two women were rescued from their stranded car in the town of Lockport. They'd been in the vehicle since 4 P M. Friday.

Across the Niagara River in Canada, four more persons were discovered in a car completely buried in snow. A passing police officer had noticed a handkerchief on a stick apparently dancing on the snow, and digging into the snowbank, he discovered an automobile containing four near-frozen motorists. Similar stories were broadcast regularly throughout the day, with the occasional news that another body had been discovered somewhere.

"Never in the memory of any living Buffalonian have we been tested by Arctic blasts as bone-chillingly brutal or as persistent in their all-time record-breaking grip as in this awesome winter of '77," said an editorial in the Buffalo *Evening News* that night. "It is a winter that no one in this region will ever forget. And now, in the midst of the worst of all winters, we must count the fearful toll of lives and property in the aftermath of the worst single storm of all, a crippling maelstrom that, for sheer ferocity, has nothing to compare with it in our frontier history."

Elsewhere, in Canada's Niagara Peninsula, 2,000 children were stranded at schools, and volunteers using snowmobiles and four-wheel drives slashed through great snowdrifts to bring the youngsters food and blankets. No attempt to remove the children would be made for days.

In northwest Ohio, hundreds of people ran out of fuel oil and were evacuated by the National Guard to emergency Red Cross shelters and other temporary quarters. In the southwestern part of the state, five young men were found dead of carbon monoxide poisoning in their snowbound car.

From northern Florida and the Gulf Coast to central Texas that night the Arctic freeze dominated. In the central and eastern states of the north, temperatures fell below zero. Yet, in Washington, Oregon, Idaho and California, the weather remained unusually warm.

President Carter called an emergency Cabinet meeting late Saturday night to deal with the devastating natural gas shortage. Someone proposed that the great quantities of gas available but unneeded in the northwest be shipped east immediately, but the President's press secretary, Jody Powell, explained that, without the emergency legislation the Congress had not yet approved, intrastate pipelines couldn't be used as a conduit for coast-to-coast shipments until extensive and time-consuming federal regulations were met.

In a mixed metaphor that pointed up the absurdity, one reporter pointed out that, for the first time in history, people might literally freeze to death in a sea of red tape.

Late that night, Mayor Makowski made an announcement: He had been on the phone with Governor Hugh Carey and his aides regularly for more than twenty-four hours, and Carey had been telephoning Washington and talking with President Carter's closest aides and top-ranking officers in the Federal Disaster Assistance Administration. As a result, said Makowski, the federal government had just issued a "declaration of emergency" in four western New York counties, including Erie. Tomorrow morning, said the mayor, Governor Hugh Carey would fly to Buffalo from New York City, and at his side would be Thomas Casey, Northeast Regional Administrator for the FDAA.

It was not the major disaster declaration Governor Carey had asked for—that would have been a more drastic measure, permitting a whole range of additional federal aid: unemployment benefits, disaster relief loans, temporary housing if necessary. One of Thomas Casey's responsibilities would be to determine whether the city should be put under such disaster status. He would come to the city tomorrow with virtual martial power to call up any branch of the federal government to provide aid for the four counties, and his office would coordinate the efforts of all branches and agencies—the Army Corps of Engineers, the National Guard, the New York Department of Transportation, the city's crews, the Red Cross, the Salvation Army, the private contractors.

The newspapers looked forward to the disaster specialist's arrival, and spoke optimistically of the pending snow blitz that would release the city from its paralysis.

*

Dispatcher Bill Strobele had an announcement, too: He told his superior that he was getting tired. He'd been working for more than thirty hours, had been awake for forty, and in two more hours he was going to quit and get some sleep. Another crew of dispatchers was due in by then anyway.

*

Late Saturday night, a guard at the Buffalo State University campus, not far from the Delaware Park Labor Camp, had an announcement also: He reported to the police that, while patrolling the campus, he had seen three full-grown reindeer gallop past him.

*

Ben Kolker at the weather station had two announcements: The day's temperature had set a new record low for the date—minus 7 degrees. Thus tumbled the old record, set in 1885.

The second announcement was the official weather forecast: "Southwesterly winds twenty to forty miles per hour with occasional higher gusts producing blowing, drifting snow and near blizzard conditions. Extreme cold, windy, with snow flurries likely."

Two more low-pressure centers had joined the one from Michigan to create a brisk flow of extremely cold air across western New York. The storm would continue into the fifth day.

19

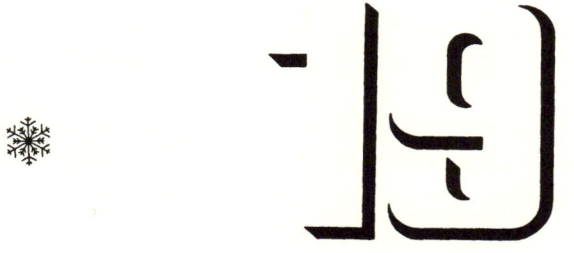

With the morning came universal optimism. In the hours after midnight, the wind and snow had slackened and Lindner's crew, along with the Department of Transportation, had opened several major roads—Main, Broadway, Michigan, Sycamore, Waldron, Fillmore, Ohio, much of South Park and Delaware. They'd also rescued two tanker trucks carrying loads of oxygen to area hospitals, and had helped a fuel oil truck to reach the Roswell Park Memorial Institute. By midmorning, defused sunlight brightened the overcast sky, with occasional moments of brilliance bursting upon the snow.

Many of those who had been stranded since Friday returned home. The storm had finally ended. And now, as the newspapers headlined and radio and TV newscasters announced hour upon hour, the federal government was stepping in immediately to get the snow removed at last. It had been a devastating winter, a simply incomprehensible storm, but it had ended, and that Sunday morning a lightness of spirit permeated the city.

*

Rose Ann Wagner sat with her mother and half a dozen still stranded customers and listened to the radio newscast. All through the previous day she'd held herself together after that moment of crying by keeping busy—she'd cooked all three meals for the men, scrubbed tables, swept, put her mind to inventing new chores and ignored the snow that relentlessly crept to impossible heights. Saturday night, after another supper of fish, the half dozen men who still could not reach their homes had played cards and told jokes, and it had seemed for those few hours that everything was as it should be again.

"Just don't think about the weather," one of the men had told her. "Think about something you like—what's your favorite food?"

Rose Ann had laughed. "Raspberry coffee cake!" she'd exclaimed.

After her husband, Matt, had phoned one last time (he'd called virtually every hour of the day), she'd gone to bed. The howl of the wind past the windows had sounded as fierce as on Friday night, and ice had glazed the entire window. For an instant, she'd fought back the fear and tears again.

Then she'd thought, "Raspberry coffee cake." Smiling to herself, she'd soon fallen asleep.

Sunday morning the frost still obliterated the bedroom window, and from the plate-glass windows of the bar she discovered that another foot of snow had fallen. Yet the sun was shining, and only a sprinkling of snow flakes fell. Soon she heard plows going by, clearing a fine path in the road.

The bar's front door opened and the man with whom she had played cards the night before stepped in, a large snow-covered bag in his arms. It had appeared to him a fine morning for a walk, he said, a little brisk perhaps, but—a miracle, it seemed!—the sun was out and the wind was letting up, too. He predicted everyone would be getting home by noon.

The phone rang. It was Matt. He'd persuaded a neighbor with a four-wheel drive to take him to Emil's. They'd pick her up before noon.

"It's over, it's over!" Rose Ann exclaimed.

"Don't go betting on it," said her mother.

The man with whom she'd played cards reached into the grocery bag and pulled out a box, handing it to her. It was a raspberry coffee cake.

"It's a miracle," he said. "I didn't think the store'd even be open, but it was. And that's the last cake on the shelf."

*

Twenty-six-year-old Rick Paine, animal keeper at the Buffalo Zoo, had reported to work to find three of the park's prize reindeer missing. A buck and two doe, one pregnant, had simply wandered across the snow that had filled the moat separating their paddock from the rest of the zoo, then up the snowbank that had buried the eight-foot chain-link fence surrounding the zoo itself, and had escaped. They'd crossed Delaware Park and the Scajaquada Expressway, and had reached the Buffalo State University campus several miles away.

At noon that Saturday, Rick and another animal keeper, twenty-three-year-old Rod Owlett, set out to find the deer in a four-wheel-drive truck. People had already called the zoo to report the animals near the Scajaquada Creek, two miles from the zoo, so Rod nudged the truck around the stalled vehicles partially blocking the entrance to the Expressway and headed west. Since the wind had abated, the men could see the frozen creek, and while Rod drove through deep drifts, Rick continuously scanned the area.

Taking another approach on the south side of the park, zoo official Jerry Aqualina and veterinarian Allen Prowton paralleled Rick's route in the doctor's van. All four men carried two-way radios to keep apprised of each other's locations. What's more, if anyone phoned the zoo to report spotting the deer, workers there would immediately convey the information by radio to the men on the road.

The farther west Rick and Rod continued, the deeper the snow became, and finally, even with all four wheels churning in the lowest gear, the hard-packed snow became an impenetrable wall at the truck's grill. The vehicle lurched, slid to the side and became locked in a snowbank. After a few futile attempts to dislodge it, the men thrust the radios into their pockets and continued on foot.

A few hundred yards farther along they spotted the deer. They were standing on the frozen creek.

"Hope that ice holds," Rick said. "It's deep there—if they go under, they'll drown, or freeze before we can get them out."

They radioed Dr. Prowton, giving the exact location of the deer. Even before they reached the animals, they saw the van bounding between the trees, across the windswept park. It stopped no more than 200 feet from the animals.

With ears twitching, the buck surveyed it. He took a few prancing steps in the opposite direction, the doe beside him. Rick Paine had positioned himself visibly in one direction, Rod Owlett in another. The buck glanced quickly at each of them and, rather than bolting, hesitated. He'd seen those people and trucks at a much closer range at the zoo, and they'd never harmed him. He had no reason to fear now.

The doctor opened the door and slowly stepped into the snow, the rifle in his hand. While the buck studied him intently, Prowton aimed the weapon.

In the silence, the crack of the 22-caliber shell seemed explosive. The buck fell under the impact of the tranquilizer dart and both doe bolted. Scrambling to his feet, the buck bounded after them. Then he fell to his knees, half rose and collapsed. Rick waited for the doe to cease their fleeing, to begin the wide circling that would eventually bring them back to the side of the fallen buck. From there it would be easy to lasso them, tie their legs and bring them back in the van. But the day had been too quiet—no traffic, no airplanes overhead, no people about, the snow muffling what few sounds might still exist. Against that silence, the shell's explosion and the buck's crashing to the ice had panicked the doe. Rick watched them streak across the park and vanish.

Rod decided to follow them on foot while the other three took the buck back to the zoo. An hour later, learning of Rod's location through the two-way radio, the four met again to plan strategy.

By then, several people had called the zoo. The animals had been spotted almost four miles away in the town of Kenmore. Someone had been chasing them on a snowmobile, and the deer had separated. Dr. Prowton said he'd try to stop the snowmobiler before the deer he was chasing died of exhaustion, and the three others set out after the other animal. For a while they continued together, but finally decided to split up and cover as many locations as possible.

At Parkside near Hertel, Rick Paine flagged down a passing police cruiser and asked for a ride to Kenmore. They were almost there when Dr. Prowton reported via the radio that he'd found the first deer. The snowmobiler had chased the animal into someone's yard where she had tried to jump a fence, fell on it and collapsed in exhaustion. A mass of people had surrounded her, tangling her in ropes, and the doctor had found her struggling, lunging futilely into the fence. He'd tranquilized her, loaded her into the van and was on his way back to the zoo, but she was suffering shock. She would not survive, the doctor predicted, nor would the fetus.

In Kenmore, Rick scoured dozens of alleys and backyards, and questioned scores of people. Hours passed, and in the cold, his hands and feet ached. The snow was beginning to blow again, settling on his glasses so that he had to wipe them frequently, and even then his vision was blurred. And he was fatigued. But he gave no thought to stopping, for with every hour, his anxiety mounted. Others would try to chase this deer, too, exhausting it or frightening it into a suicidal lunge that would lead to broken legs or neck. The deer's enemies were not the elements—it could live on the small twigs and roughage it would find in the snow, even on the bark of trees. And, unlike most animals, a deer's hair is hollow, providing efficient insulation. Its enemies were those few people who, perhaps with good intentions (perhaps not), used brawn instead of brain to capture the animal. Breaking into a jog, sometimes slipping and stumbling, he continued through the town.

Another call on the radio suggested the deer had been seen in a distant neighborhood. Rick flagged down the next vehicle he saw and hitched another ride. Twenty minutes later, he was on foot again.

Late in the afternoon, a police car approached.

"You with the zoo?" the officer asked, staring at the insignia on Rick's jacket.

"Right—you see the deer?"

"Get in—it's in somebody's yard."

A minute later, Rick confronted the animal. She stood in the center of the yard, breathing hard and resting, her eyes still wide with terror. Behind her was a long, narrow shed, the back wall against the rear fence. The space between the building and the fence along the right side of the yard created a five-foot-wide paddock, and Rick realized that if he could coax the deer into it he would have a chance to hold her there until the doctor came with his tranquilizer dart.

First he called the doctor, Jerry and Rod on the two-way radio. Then, very cautiously, he entered the yard.

Even under the best of circumstances deer are flighty and unpredictable creatures, facing one direction, darting in another, now at rest, now in full flight, one instant hurling like an arrow, the next zigzagging like a rabbit. Rick realized that at the slightest provocation she might easily sail over the fence and be gone. Still, she appeared exhausted. She'd need some reserve for the leap. He stepped toward her. The deer stepped back, then turned.

It was too late, Rick realized with despair. At the far side of the yard, toward which the deer was moving, a drift had formed as high as the fence. She would simply walk over it, just as she had at the zoo. He ran, hoping to circle around her. If she hesitated, he would have a chance to cut her off at the drift, and although she could outrun him, she might not attempt it, might spin back into the yard, past the shed and into the corral.

But she didn't hesitate. Instead, she bolted straight for the drift with Rick twenty feet behind. He watched her gather herself for the lunge and flight.

Instead, she sank into the snow. It seemed impossible, for the wind had packed the drifts as solid as ice. Yet, the doe foundered up to her breast. Rick ran toward her, but she scrambled free to dart past him, heading toward the gate through which she'd entered the yard.

The neighbors milling there frightened her and she swerved, racing between the shed and the fence. No drift had gathered here, and the fence surprised her. With too little space to gather herself for the leap, she spun around, starting back into the yard.

Rick was there. She tried to pass him, but he threw his arms around her neck. She twisted, bucked, but he held on and finally wrestled her to the ground. For a moment she continued struggling, but he held her down firmly until she finally quieted, her head locked in his arm and cushioned from the snow by his body.

A moment later, Jerry arrived.

For forty-five minutes, with the temperature only a few degrees above zero and the snow falling steadily, Rick and Jerry held the doe. Neighbors brought them hot cocoa, but their hands were too stiff to hold the cup; someone lifted it to their lips.

When the doctor arrived, he tranquilized the deer. The pregnant doe had died, he said. But this one looked healthy. She'd live.

Rick had one more assignment that day. It was almost 4 P.M. when he returned to the zoo to learn that Mamie, the huge African elephant, had developed a serious ear infection with fever, chills and loss of appetite. She needed an injection of antibiotics. But in the past, Mamie had proven temperamental—she'd tried to throw a few of the keepers through the wall. Among them she considered only Rick Paine her friend. He alone would go into her cage.

That afternoon, talking softly to the great animal, caressing her, Rick injected the antibiotic. He coaxed her to eat some food, offering it by hand, and she assented.

'20

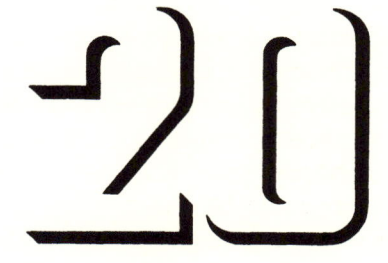

At noon Sunday, as Rick Paine and Rod Owlett were setting out to locate the deer, New York Governor Hugh Carey and Federal Disaster Assistance Administrator northeast coordinator Thomas Casey arrived at Buffalo International Airport with a sizable contingent of state and federal officials. They flew in on a C-130 cargo transport that also carried several pieces of heavy-duty snow removal equipment. Mayor Makowski and other local officials were on hand to greet the dignitaries and hold a brief closed-door meeting with Colonel Michael Sullivan, Jr., of the National Guard. Then the entourage of politicians, reporters and hangers-on climbed into ten cars, one bus and one helicopter and proceeded to City Hall.

There, photographs were the first order: Makowski and Carey posed in the snow of Niagara Square; Casey and Carey chatted amiably; County Executive Ed Regan, Deputy Buffalo Mayor Les Foschio—even the sheriff—were photographed.

Governor Carey praised the city's resilience. "The spirit and morale of people here has been just splendid," he said. "We'll carry on—and here comes the federal government." Coordinator Casey then held another meeting with local officials in the Management Information Center near the mayor's second-floor office.

There was some confusion that afternoon regarding just where Mr. Casey would set up his operations. The Mayor and his staff had anticipated that Casey would work out of Management Information Center in City Hall, but that idea was dismissed immediately—

Casey had not come to serve merely the city of Buffalo, he said. Adjourning the City Hall meeting, he immediately called another in the Rath Erie County Building nearby. There, he met with representatives of the Red Cross, the Salvation Army, DOT disaster coordinator Ed Janak and his boss, Dave Piper, representatives of the Army Corps of Engineers, the Department of Energy, the Civil Defense and others. Casey barred city and county officials and the press from that gathering, but they missed little. Casey simply explained the plan of attack: Everyone would continue doing what he or she had been doing. The city of Buffalo, its suburbs and the county would continue to feed to the New York Department of Transportation lists of roads in need of clearing. DOT would assign the work orders, not only to its own crews, but now also to the Army Corps of Engineers. The Corps would immediately set about making contracts with local private individuals and firms to fulfill the requests coming from DOT. These contracts would be made verbally and the paperwork taken care of later. DOT would also give assignments to the National Guard.

The position of DOT disaster coordinator for New York's western counties thus became pivotal. National attention would focus on it, and credit for the imminent opening of the city would center upon that focal point. It was therefore decided that Ed Janak would step aside, and his boss, Dave Piper, would assume the DOT coordination leadership. In fact, Janak would continue to serve, but not as figurehead.

Casey himself would oversee the whole affair. City and county officials were to determine the amount of equipment they needed to do a more effective job, and he would supply it. He'd plug any holes, keep the rusty gears turning, sand off the burrs in the lines of communication. If necessary, he'd call in the army with additional heavy equipment.

Commented Mayor Makowski, "A strategy has been devised and we will be getting immediate action."

The first action was that, within a few hours, Tom Casey moved to another building again. The Rath Building, an aide explained, was a county structure, but Casey was there to aid *all* of western New York. Thus, it was more appropriate that he set up headquarters at Donovan, a state office building. The telephone company, which had already installed a bank of phones in the Rath Building, now sent its hard-pressed workers to do the same at Donovan. That day, they installed a total of sixty-three sets in the two buildings.

That afternoon, under clear skies, thousands of residents shoveled their way out of their homes and explored the city. A parade of sightseers, some on foot but most in automobiles, snaking along the single lanes that Lindner's crews had cleared, swarmed into the downtown area.

Taking advantage of a road that the Buffalo *Evening News* had plowed clear in order to make newspaper deliveries, the Brinks Company sent some men in a four-wheel drive to the newspaper office to rescue the guards and money.

*

At 3 P.M., a new wind came from the west, carrying fresh snow. The sky grew dark with its density, and many of the sightseers returned home immediately. Thousands, familiar with the region's brief squalls, continued on their way, stopping only when poor visibility made any movement treacherous. But the snow continued with increasing severity, and before long hundreds were stranded, their vehicles once more blocking the major roads.

Again, the city's handful of dilapidated tow trucks were put to work. The crippled plows manned by exhausted crews offered yet another feeble challenge to the accumulating snow.

By eight o'clock that night, a changed consciousness had descended upon the people of Buffalo and surrounding counties. At the time, few articulated it. Yet, from the East Side slums to the elegant estates of the north, from the busy complaint desk of the South Park precinct to the corridors of City Hall, almost everyone sensed the change. Even children who, earlier in the day, had frolicked in the sunshine, grew thoughtful; thousands of homes had run out of milk, hundreds had no food.

For many who had calmly endured, the blizzard's return marked the beginning of fear, even dread. There were those who would suffer emotional breakdowns because of the storm's return, others who would leave a lifetime of friends and relatives to relocate elsewhere rather than risk another such confrontation.

At 8 P.M., Red Cross officials, aware that the National Weather Service predicted no clearing trend, organized a convoy of trucks and, following routes that had been kept clear, directed it to one of the nearby wholesale food terminals. The supplies were brought to the Red Cross headquarters on Delaware Avenue, and from there they were delivered to emergency shelters and thousands of needy families.

At the same time the convoy started out to the food terminal, National Guardsmen and equipment poured from the Connecticut Street Armory to join Lindner's crews in an initial attempt at snow removal—the plan to start Monday had been moved up a day on the governor's orders. Two trucks that had been promised hadn't arrived, but the cold weather gear had, and the typical guardsman resembled an astronaut, so well hidden was he beneath his clothing. He wore rubber boots over combat boots, heavy socks, long johns, jeans, fatigues, Army cold-weather trousers, T-shirt, sweatshirt, fatigue shirt, scarf, Army parka with hood and liner, perhaps a beanie and gloves. Many had smeared their faces with petroleum jelly to protect them from frostbite.

Still, the front-end loaders had not been designed for winter use, so the cabs were not enclosed. The trucks had no heaters. And the windchill factor that night fell to a minus 40 degrees. To prevent frostbite and freezing, the men operating the open equipment were ordered to work in no longer than fifteen-minute shifts, and the truck drivers were encouraged to take frequent breaks.

The Guard's major assignment that night was to assist Lindner's crews in clearing access roads to the city's hospitals. Since Friday afternoon, those needing emergency treatment had been forced to walk several blocks to reach most hospitals. Volunteers had carried others on stretchers, and a few had been airlifted by helicopter. Now the Guard and city crews dug the snow from those roads, loaded it on trucks and dumped it in nearby parks, playgrounds and parking lots. In many areas, neighbors invited the men into their homes, offering them dry clothes, coffee, soup, sandwiches—even warm brandy.

*

The Red Bessie also made the rounds that night. A wornout 1951 Ford van that had been converted to a diner on wheels, the Red Bessie was the Buffalo Salvation Army's only canteen. In addition to food and hot beverages, it toted a supply of emergency clothing, gloves, hats, scarves and such. That night, the Red Bessie puttered from hospital to hospital to distribute food and clothing until finally, with frozen windshield wipers, steaming radiator and smoking engine, it broke down. Within half an hour, a city tow truck arrived, hoisted the Red Bessie and for the rest of the night towed it to the work locations.

*

Although most of those stranded on Friday had returned home, the Statler Hotel on Niagara Square continued to do a thriving business. In addition to Sunday afternoon's newly snowbound, an army of out-of-town politicians, officials, assistants and assistants to assistants had checked in. Others who lived in Buffalo and were needed downtown but were unable to commute also stayed at the hotel. Ed Janak was one of those. So was Mike McKeating, a reporter for the Buffalo *Evening News*. For most of the night, McKeating had made the hotel bar his beat, and among his many casual observations was that Thomas Casey, the FDAA northeastern disaster coordinator, had once again changed offices, this time to the Statler bar. Earlier in the evening, Casey had told the press he had no time for interviews, for he was busy arranging snow removal contracts with private firms. In fact, he had delegated that responsibility to Colonel Daniel D. Ludwig of the U.S. Army Corps of Engineers, and Ludwig in turn had given the assignment to Henry Vitale, the district's emergency operations planner. Before Vitale himself could undertake anything, he had to be transported from his home to the Army Corps headquarters by snowmobile, for the Army Corps property, fronting Lake Erie on north Niagara Street, was probably the most overwhelmed and inaccessible area of the city.

In order that there might be something for the press to photograph, Casey had instructed Ludwig, who had instructed Vitale, to get at least one contractor working by Monday. Vitale had immediately put to work many of those who had been stranded at the Corps offices since Friday, having them telephone contractors with heavy earthmoving and hauling equipment—the mountains of snow had packed like ice, rendering plows and graders useless. According to Casey's instructions, the contractors would be paid an hourly rate that would vary according to the type of equipment they supplied, and an Army Corps representative would be assigned to every work site to assure that the job was being done efficiently.

Such were the instructions that had filtered down to Hank Vitale. Implementing them, however, proved virtually impossible that Sunday night—almost no contractors could be reached at their work numbers; those who were there didn't have adequate equipment; those who did couldn't get it started; those who could didn't have the crews to operate it.

Vitale had an assistant prepare a special bulletin requesting private contractors who might be of assistance to contact the Army

Corps. By telephone, Vitale's staff gave the message to the city's radio and television stations, and it was broadcast frequently during the night. Still, there was little response.

Late that night, Casey learned that a single crew would indeed go to work late Monday afternoon—just one—on South Park Avenue near the city line.

Federal snow-removal equipment was already enroute to western New York, Casey assured McKeating in the Statler bar that night. However, the full impact of the federal efforts would not become visible until Tuesday, he explained.

*

Across vast sections of Ohio, western Pennsylvania and New York the wind roared, visibility dropped to zero and incalculable tons of snow clogged the roads so laboriously cleared hours earlier. James Lindner sat alone in his office at the Broadway Garage and stared at the opaque window. All the sacrifice had been for nothing. Yet, even now, even against impossible odds, they continued plowing those hospital entrances. They couldn't endure much longer, the streets crews, police and firemen, the hundreds of volunteers, the lonely stranded, those in unheated homes, without food. He wondered how many hundreds still lay dead in their cars, how many cars remained buried, perhaps not to be discovered until weeks hence when a plow finally reached them.

In outlying counties near Buffalo, he'd learned, drifts were rising higher than ever, and in some locales, authorities had not only banned traffic but snowmobiles—one snowmobiler had been injured when he collided with a rooftop chimney, and others had narrowly missed electrocution while skimming along snowbanks as high as utility pole electric wires.

From Texas to Florida that night snow and rain swept the country, and weather stations from Canada to the Gulf warned of continuing Arctic cold.

PART III

There may now exist great men for things that do not exist. —Jacob Burckhardt

21

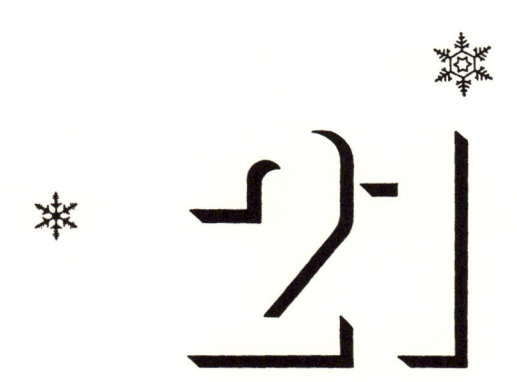

The snow line at the equator is 17,000–18,000 feet; in England and America, 5,000; and at the poles it is at sea level. At those altitudes, the air is always cold. The temperature, even in summer, hovers near the freezing point, permitting little thaw of the winter's snow. Thus, in areas of high precipitation, the snow gathers age upon age and accumulates in deep and sweeping snowfields from the high middle latitudes to the poles.

As the new snow falls upon the old, the weight of it packs the underlying crystals ever more tightly until they appear a solid, glass-like mountain of ice. Their individual forms seem to dissolve in the glacial mass, but it is an illusion, and as the enormous weight of the titanic mounds shift, the individual crystals begin with exquisite slowness to slide out from under the pressure. As a bag of marbles beneath the weight of a man's foot might burst at a weak seam and the marbles roll down a flight of steps to the lowest point, so the ice crystals, pressed beneath the weight of eternal snowfalls might split a granite mountain and flow toward a lower point. The moving crystals form a river of ice, a glacier, cracking continents, slashing the land, hollowing it.

The world's great climate cycle is of heat and ice. In the beginning, after the conflagration and melting, the dark clouds of smoke and steam enveloped the earth in a shield impenetrable by the sun's rays, and the cold advanced. The Keewaton, first of a dozen Ice Ages, descended some five thousand million years ago. Once every three hundred million years, the ice apparently gains dominion over the earth again. Within the aeons of the great cycle are subcycles, eras of cold, the glacial phases, and the interglacials. Each lasts about seventy-five thousand years.

It may be that we are still in the twelfth Ice Age, the Pleistocene, the million-year-old epoch during which the earth has endured four glaciations. We bask today in an interglacial phase, expected to continue about fifty thousand years longer.

The last glacial period, the Wisconsin Glaciation, began with a gradual cooling some seventy-five thousand years ago. For twenty thousand years, the snow fell and pressed into ice, the ice weighing heavier and heavier upon the earth, rising like a mountain until, all over the northern part of the sphere, the individual crystals slipped inperceptibly forward, an inch, a foot, not more than two feet a year, snow crystals in number greater than the sand grains of all the ocean floors, beyond calculation, beyond meaning.

From many directions the ice oozed south, chilling the air, sucking moisture from it in furious blizzards on which the glaciers continued to nourish. For fifteen thousand years, the glaciers covered all of Canada and the United States as far south as Kentucky. They cut deep into the south central states, swept east to Long Island, buried Buffalo, buried Ireland and most of England. Scandinavia was covered with a solid ice cap more than a mile thick and thousands of square miles wide. Ice covered Russia to the Urals, blanketed eastern Asia. All of northern Europe was an unbroken ice cap.

With the descending cold, glaciers formed in the mountains of the equator. Snow fell in South America and in the deserts of Africa.

All across the earth, the air surrendered its moisture in Herculean gales of snow and rain, forming an inland sea over most of Utah, Nevada and Idaho. Lakes appeared in the world's deserts.

The water of those lakes and the ice that crowned the earth and the rain that drove upon it and the snow that fell without ceasing for a thousand centuries came from the sea. The oceans' depths dropped by 200 meters and new land appeared everywhere. The Bering Strait became a broad, flat, tree-covered plain. An ice bridge joined Australia and Tasmania. The Baltic was a small bowl of ice.

The Wisconsin Glaciation lasted seventy-five thousand years, ending only a hundred centuries ago. Many creatures perished; a few endured, living on the brutal tundra and ice that covered a third of the earth. Many were small, furry animals, but there were also caribou and wolves and mastodons and woolly mammoths, and man, who had long before lost any fur he might have had. The mammoths and the mastodons grew extinct, but man survived, hurled himself, puny and naked, against those awesome beasts, wrapped his body in their skins, filled his stomach with their flesh. He alone of the higher life forms had neither fur nor feathers but, like the bison, he huddled with his kind against the elements and he survived. Man survived.

22

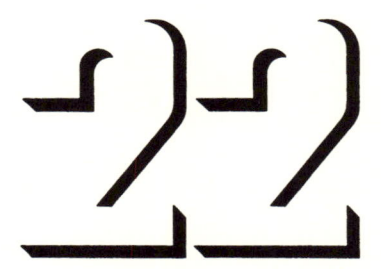

Jeff Hensey awakened shivering in his law office south of City Hall Monday morning. The heat in the building had been set low for the weekend, and the small electric space heater he'd found near the secretary's desk had all but lost the battle to the cold.

He sat up immediately, ignoring the pain in his shoulders and arms, the result of two days of unprecedented physical activity. For a moment he sat motionless, fighting his way to complete wakefulness, trying to formulate a plan of action. He would move the heater to the tiny restroom, turn on the coffeemaker in the secretary's office, take his spare suit and his shaving kit to the restroom, wait for the room to warm up, strip naked and wash with paper towels in the sink, bask in the warm air blowing over his body, shave, comb his hair, dress in the fresh suit, pour a cup of hot coffee and bring it back into the restroom, sit on the toilet and drink it in relaxed leisure.

While the coffee perked and the restroom warmed, Jeff stood near the window and watched the snow fall in Niagara Square. The wind had abated again—since Saturday morning there had been periods of profound stillness such as this, the snow falling like a curtain of delicate lace. On Saturday morning, on the snowmobile, he had bounded through just such a snowfall, delivering drugs from Emergency Hospital, bringing a nurse to work (she'd agreed to meet him later, but he'd forgotten), carrying supplies to the Louisiana Street precinct, finally transporting officers to the lakefront to search stranded cars for dead motorists.

Late that night, he'd traveled the several miles from south Buffalo to the Salvation Army on North Main Street to answer a plea for more snowmobiles, and he'd awakened Sunday morning on the floor in a corner of the Golden Age Club facilities, glanced through a window and was momentarily blinded by a burst of sunlight off the snow. It lasted only a minute before a new flutter of snow descended.

The Army's headquarters had all but emptied by noon. Jeff himself had driven home a few of the more daring elderly who had been stranded since Friday—one seventy-two-year-old woman, clinging to him with both arms as the snowmobile leaped over the drifts, shouted in his ear that she'd never had so much fun in her life. He'd helped her up the steps to her apartment, and, opening her change purse, she'd pulled one dollar from the two or three she had folded there.

"Nothing doing, sweetie," Jeff insisted. "I'm the one who should be paying you—it was a *hell* of a blast."

The old woman patted his cheek. There was a moment when she seemed without words. Then she reached up and, pulling his head toward her, planted a kiss on his forehead.

"You be good," she said. "And stop by any old time."

He had intended to return home that afternoon, but Captains Banfield and Williams of the Salvation Army had kept him busy delivering food and other necessities, and then, at 3 P M , the wind had risen again, driving the snow into new drifts, limiting vision.

Still, he'd wanted to go home. He'd called his wife, Midge, frequently on Saturday; so often, in fact, that she'd finally questioned him about it, for she'd assured him that the children were fine, actually out on the lawn attempting to build a snowman—unsuccessfully, since the snow was too cold to pack.

"I miss you, that's all," he'd said. He couldn't have explained the feeling—his body, his emotions, were drained; too little sleep, an overwhelming enemy in the storm, so many people pleading for help that only a relatively few would be reached. Instead of satisfaction at the missions accomplished, he felt only despair over the impossible number remaining.

He needed comfort, petting, mothering, something secure in contrast to this endlessly swirling, ever-changing landscape. He imagined the orange and yellow brilliance of the fireplace at home, his children, his wife.

Sunday afternoon, he'd returned the snowmobile to his brother, whom he then persuaded to drive him downtown to his office, from where he would be able to reach his car and return home as soon as the roads were clear. Late Sunday night, he'd trudged across Niagara Square to the Statler Hotel, ordered his first good meal since dinner Thursday night and had two drinks in the hotel bar. He hadn't recognized Thomas Casey or any of the other important people there, and if he had, it wouldn't have mattered to him. He was too weary and disgusted.

He stumbled back to his office Sunday night in a half-intoxicated stupor, stopping in the middle of the empty square to, like Captain Ahab, curse grandly the forces of nature. His words were swept away by the wind.

With resolute anger, he had retired to his office.

As he watched the snowfall Monday morning, he refused to be deceived. The lulls would give way again to the eternal blizzard. He pondered for a moment just how long the storm could conceivably continue. The great blizzard of 1888 had struck on March 11—could the wind, cold and snow actually continue until March, making mere survival a grim and perpetual chore, destroying tens of thousands through freezing and starvation?

If he could only reach home, they could manage even without fuel—he'd tack the insulated drapes from the second floor across the center of the living room to make a small survival area near the fireplace. When the firewood was gone, he'd tear out the second-floor walls and burn the studs—they'd be less expensive to replace than the quality furniture. He'd even rip the floorboards up, and finally, if it came to it, the dining room chairs and table, twelve hundred dollars' worth of kindling. And he'd leave the water running in the toilet bowl and kitchen sink—to hell with the other pipes.

The sound of the coffee steaming interrupted his thoughts, and Jeff set about preparing himself for the day. An hour later, feeling more like an attorney than he had in almost a week, he left the office and went to the Statler for breakfast. There, perhaps, he would learn of the status of the roads south. If possible, he'd get the Oldsmobile started and head home immediately.

An atmosphere of tension permeated the hotel's coffee shop. Department of Transportation employees huddled in one section, Casey's federal aides in another. City Hall officials conversed with county personnel in somber tones. Among those in the latter group was Matt Quinby of Erie County Executive Edward Regan's office.

Jeff hailed him: "Eggs and sausage?"

Matt shrugged.

Prologue *In the weeks prior to January 28, 1977—the day of the great blizzard—such scenes as this were routine Snow flurries fell continually, approaches to major highways were often jammed*
(Buffalo Evening News/Robert L Smith)

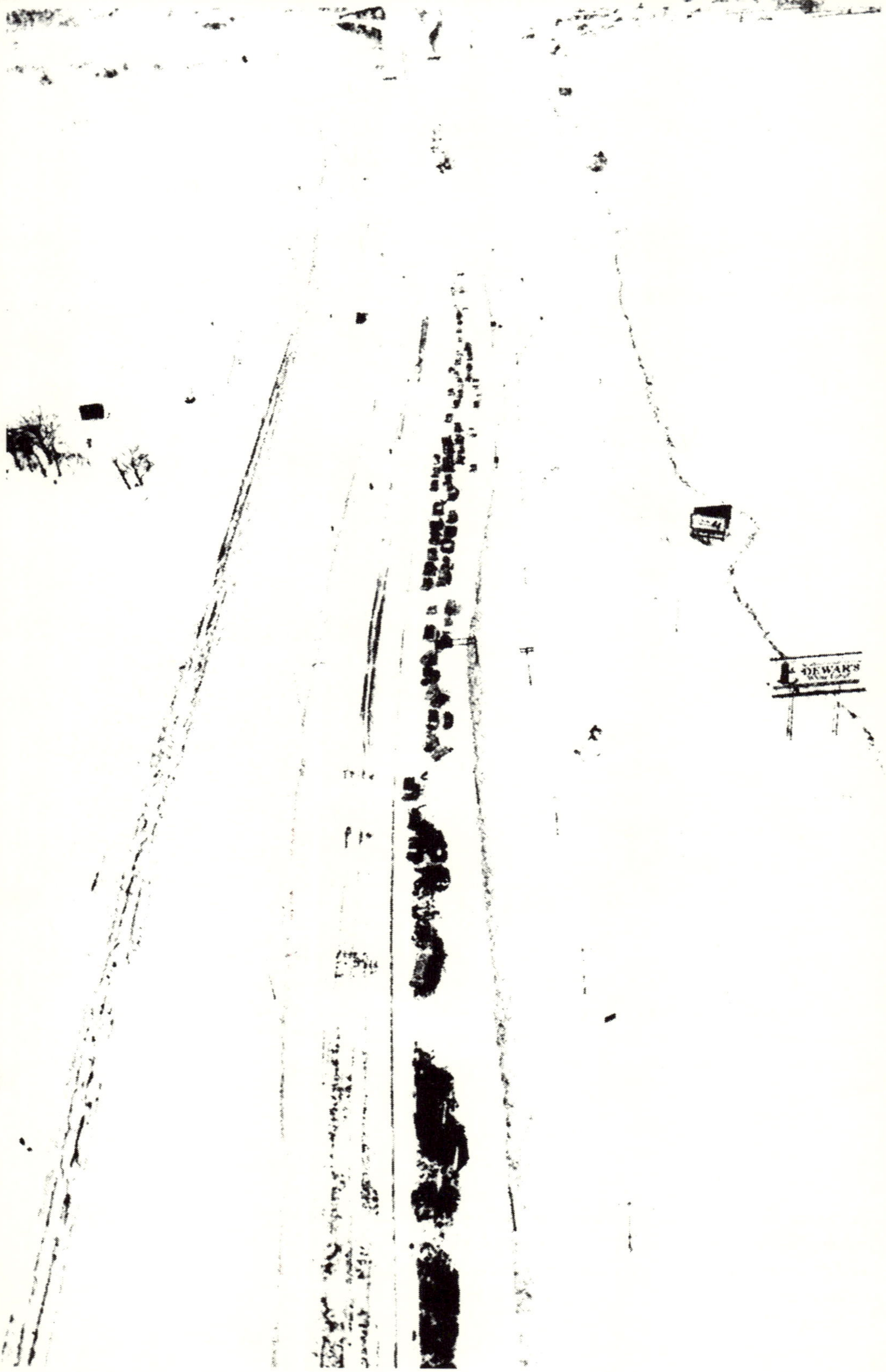
DEWAR'S

Sunday night, January 30, the Buffalo branch of the Salvation Army's only canteen, the Red Bessie, hit the streets. A few hours later, the old girl broke down, and had to be towed to various work sites. In the following days, however, modern canteens like these arrived in Buffalo from throughout the state. They provided not only food and beverages, but gloves, scarfs, and other necessities to National Guardsmen and others who worked twelve-hour shifts in windchill factors of minus fifty degrees and more. (Salvation Army Buffalo Headquarters)

The morning before. This is how Fuhrmann Boulevard appeared on Thursday morning, January 27, the day before the blizzard. Hours earlier, Paul Dengler and Jeff Hensey, along with more than one hundred others, were taken to shelter in emergency vehicles that reached them in the cleared left lane. The shore of Lake Erie is visible to the right of the billboard.
(Buffalo Evening News/Richard W. Roeller)

While the blizzard brought most modern transportation to a halt, enterprising youngsters Kim Dipirro and her brother, Dwayne, found travel easy once the wind abated. The family's pet sled-pulling malamute even had an advantage over the snowmobiles —a sense of direction that helped Kim find her way home during periods of poor visibility.
(Courier-Express/*Ron Schifferle*)

We can make it if we help each other.
(Courier-Express/*Ron Moscati*)

Volunteer snowmobilers such as these who worked with the Red Cross saved scores of lives. Discovering a flag planted in the snow, these two men dig to find a buried car. (Buffalo Evening News/*Robert L. Smith*)

Some western New York farms were virtually wiped out. Cattle starved when farmers couldn't reach them. Barn roofs collapsed. Farmers couldn't get the milk out of their own driveways, much less to the terminals, and had to dump it. (Buffalo Evening News/ *Richard W. Roeller*)

William Bellis and his crew lift off in the "Huey" chopper enroute to Bradford, Pennsylvania, and a critically ill infant in need of emergency treatment. (Courier-Express/*Ron Shifferle*)

In removing thousands of cars from the Buffalo streets, tow truck drivers created temporary parking lots wherever they could find the space As the two cars on the right illustrate, some towers gave more priority to haste than to finesse
(Buffalo Evening News/Ronald J Colleran)

A few blocks from Emil's Inn, where Rose Ann Wagner spent three days, volunteers use a trenching machine and shovels to create an entrance to a buried home The effort to dig out Mr and Mrs Robert Thompson required moving twenty truckloads of snow (Buffalo Evening News/ Ronald J Colleran)

With heroic efforts, firefighters join neighbors in the all but impossible attempt to
control the Whitney Place holocaust. Watching in despair as five houses blaze,
one man kneels to pray. (Joe Paul Falzone)

A young man clears the sidewalk in front of Main Place Mall, blowing the snow into Washington Street. A few hours earlier, city plows had pushed the snow from the street onto the sidewalk. Only after the January 28 blizzard, was priority given to removing the snow rather than piling it in ever-expanding banks along the curb. (Buffalo Evening News/ Barney Kerr)

Mayor Stanley Makowski (second from left) greets the 3 A M arrival of an Air Force C-5 Galaxy from New York City. The plane carried four huge snowblowers, two utility trucks, a scoop loader and a scout vehicle, loaned to Buffalo by New York City's Mayor Abraham D. Beame.
(Buffalo Evening News/Ronald J. Colleran)

The remains of this 1972 vehicle were discovered three months after the blizzard. Along with mountains of snow removed from the city's streets, the vehicle was apparently lifted by a giant bulldozer, dumped along with the snow into a huge truck, and transported to LaSalle Park, to be found in mid-April when the snow melted. (Buffalo Evening News/Dennis C. Enser)

"Scrambled?"

He shrugged again, turned grimly to his colleagues to add a few more words, then sauntered to Jeff's table.

"You look like somebody took off with your wife," Jeff said.

"I should be so lucky."

Matt Quinby virtually collapsed in a chair and ordered the first waitress who passed to bring him a cup of coffee. He'd been at the Rath Building all night, he said, sleeping for a few hours at his desk and spending the rest of the time preparing a clear overview of the "situation," as he called it—"not solutions, understand—just some kind of picture of the whole goddamn problem."

There were still loose ends, scores of them no doubt, but the one indisputable point was that the city was falling apart. This was no San Francisco earthquake, no Chicago fire, no Galveston flood, but it was a disaster just the same, and people years from now would be talking about the Buffalo blizzard.

The Sewer and Water Department expected underground pipes to freeze and burst any minute. Towns all over Erie County and elsewhere had declared emergencies and banned all but emergency travel. Cheektowaga had hired private firms to clear the streets yesterday, but all but a few had been blown closed again overnight. The fire department there was checking houses snow-covered to their roofs to make sure nobody was freezing or suffocating.

Mrs. Gayle Syposs, acting mayor of Tonawanda, was complaining that some of her men had been working on the roads for thirty-six straight hours and all her efforts to get some federal and state crews and equipment to the town had failed.

Town of Clarence supervisor Wallace Gibson had told the police to ticket all motorists, and authorized the fire department to confiscate gasoline if necessary to prevent driving in the town.

Only two north-south routes were open in Lancaster, and the supervisor, Stanley Keysa, was furious that his requests for federal and state assistance had netted him one broken-down snowplow.

Wind conditions had proven so severe in Newseat that some drifts had reached about thirty feet. Even emergency snowmobile service had to be cut for fear the vehicles would hit electric utility lines.

In some towns, crews were using metal detectors to find cars buried beneath the snow before attacking the drifts with massive equipment. Erie County Sheriff Ken Braun had toured the area by helicopter early Sunday and near Lancaster had spotted 125 cars and

147

trucks almost completely buried. He noticed one young man standing on a snowdrift and leaning against a street light suspended across the intersection.

Nearby Niagara Falls had become a virtual ghost town.

Jeff asked about Hamburg.

"Same as every place else," said Quinby. "They got private contractors down there, but what can you do? It's that damn wind." After a moment he added, "Oh, they'll be all right, long as they can find a place to put the garbage for a week. Nobody's picking up any garbage. They got South Park open down there, but try getting outta Buffalo."

Jeff sipped his coffee thoughtfully. Finally he said, "Well, I'm gonna see if I can make it."

"Lotsa luck. I'll be here for drinks at five. Stop by."

*

The Oldsmobile wouldn't start—snow had blown under the hood, caking around the spark plugs and distributor cap. But even if it had started, a drift blocked the exit ramp, and although all the stalled cars had been towed, Jeff could see that many streets had blown closed again.

Disgusted, he trudged back to his office, called Midge to tell her where he was, talked to the children. Then, in coat and boots, he sat at his desk and buried himself in *Corpus Jurisprudence*.

*

The morning quickly became a symphony of discord, with disheartening notes struck from every corner. Postmaster William Miller had announced the day before that mail deliveries would begin on schedule Monday morning, although seventy jeeps were still stranded on Buffalo streets and little mail had arrived from out of town. Still, thousands of people would be awaiting welfare and railroad retirement checks, and Miller expected to get them out.

But on Monday morning, a spokesman for the Buffalo Post Office confessed that deliveries would not be made after all, although perhaps by Tuesday at least some mail might be sorted and delivered to substations and branches. People who desperately needed their checks might find a way to their local substation and pick them up there.

The post office was not alone in its immobility. The Niagara Frontier Transit Metro System had tried to keep a few buses running Monday morning on the handful of main arteries that were clear— these for use by those who absolutely had to travel, such as firemen, policemen, and medical personnel. Still, of the more than four hundred buses the system usually had in service, only twenty were operating Monday—and on nothing remotely resembling a schedule.

Still, Niagara Frontier could boast more success than the intercity bus lines; since Friday, neither Trailways nor Greyhound had accomplished any movement in or out of their terminals. Amtrak reported frozen cars, frozen tracks, and continued cancellations. At the airport, only a few private planes had taken off.

The National Fuel Gas Company offered the particularly unwelcome news that, because weather forecasters saw no relief in sight from the severe cold, and because gas supplies were more critical than ever, the company was curtailing all gas except for amounts sufficient to prevent freezing to its industrial and commercial customers for the entire coming week. The company would begin monitoring industrial and commercial customers immediately, and would promptly cut all service to those ignoring the order. It was essential to assure sufficient gas to residential customers.

*

Tom Casey's offices in the Donovan Building Monday morning appeared chaotic. Western New York had been divided into districts—counties, villages, cities and such. Each was to make its requests for aid directly to the New York State Department of Transportation coordinator assigned to it, but few officials in the many districts understood that, and much of the day was spent redirecting pleas for assistance to the proper coordinators.

Even when authorities made their requests to the designated DOT coordinator, little could be done, however. The Army Corps still had only one contractor willing to begin work Monday.

Nor could Casey expect much immediate help from the National Guard. While the entire 152nd Engineer Battalion and elements of the 42nd Aviation Battalion and the 221st Engineers group had been mobilized, bringing more than five hundred Guardsmen to the Connecticut Street Armory, the amount of work they could accomplish was limited by their equipment—five front-end loaders and a few bulldozers to keep one hundred trucks busy. The Guardsmen were working hard; they'd opened some important routes and had kept access roads to the city's hospitals clear. They'd also provided forty jeeps for emergency missions. Still, neither the Guards nor anyone else was performing the miracle the politicians and the public had expected of Tom Casey and the federal government. The snow was still falling; the roads remained generally unusable.

149

In response to the continuing clamor for action, Tom Casey announced that he would bring in still additional personnel: 300 U.S. Army soldiers from an engineer battalion at Fort Bragg, North Carolina. They would fly into Buffalo, he said, "as soon as they can get here," although nobody ventured to guess what they might do once they arrived.

Casey faced another problem Monday afternoon: In response to his request the day before, six city departments submitted a list of their needs in combating the blizzard. It included:

—Department of General Services: 35 four-wheel drive vehicles, 15 high-lifts, 1,000 sets of chains, service contracts to repair motor vehicles, auto parts valued at $35,000, 1,500 shovels, 20 snowmobiles, 2,000 hot meals a day, a field hospital, medical supplies, more than a hundred workers, 1,000 warm gloves, towing chains, red warning flags and flares.

—The Fire Department: 12 pumpers, 3 aerial ladders, 6 panel trucks, 4 jeeps, 60 portable radios, 90 sets of chains, generators, propane thawers, 300 sections of fire hose, 29 nozzles, 20 axes and a mobile canteen.

—Department of Parks: 15 generators, 6,000 gallons of fuel oil and 15 four-wheel drive vehicles.

—Department of Police: 20 four-wheel drive vehicles, 8 tow trucks, a bulldozer, gasoline, 14 snowmobiles and operators, 50 sets of car chains and 50 jumper cables.

—Department of Streets and Sanitation: 190 trucks, 60 high-lifts, 10 blowers, 40 tow trucks, 8 bulldozers, 20 plows, 100 sets of chains, 250 shovels, 500 flares, 250 fluorescent flags and 10 portable radios.

—Department of Transportation: a signal trouble truck, 24 jumper cables, a dozen bullhorns, a dozen portable radios and many four-wheel drive vehicles.

In a cover letter, the mayor explained that the list was as "comprehensive as possible" but additional needs might arise later.

*

A light snow continued falling throughout the day, and the wind alternately ebbed and rushed, sometimes gusting to more than forty miles per hour. News people from local media, national wire services and the networks scurried across the city searching for new angles to the week's biggest story, the six-day blizzard, the storm that had crippled one of the nation's great cities.

Most of the stories concentrated on the invisible war machine that the federal government was assembling to conquer the elements, while others described items of human interest: Two thugs attacked a seventy-one-year-old man struggling through the snow and robbed him of nineteen dollars; another man knocked a Salvation Army volunteer off his snowmobile while he was delivering food to shut-ins and stole the machine. For some hours thereafter, the wind and snow ceased, permitting the police to follow the snowmobile tracks to the thief's house.

While the news media continued to uncover fresh drama, hundreds of thousands of western New Yorkers found Monday to be the longest day of that interminable winter. It was barren of both the awesome majesty of raging elements, and the flicker of sunlight that on Sunday had offered the illusion of deliverance. The day hung like a fog, desolate and without movement, hours drifting into each other without distinction.

A spirit of despair pervaded the city. People grew quarrelsome, but even in disputing they invested no emotion. Sitting at their windows, they gazed trancelike at the snow and thought of nothing.

Jeff Hensey had worked furiously all day, drawing the curtains and refusing to allow himself a moment's thought about the weather. Thus, he'd accomplished a great deal, and that had lifted his spirits. At 5 P.M., he rewarded himself by throwing wide the drapes, making another cup of coffee and sitting by the window, coat still tightly buttoned, to ponder the landscape. In the glow of the streetlights, the snow semed to wash across the vast square in long, flowing waves. It decorated the sculptured lions at the base of the monument in the square's center with an unbroken flange out of which the column itself seemed to spring. Across the street, where hours before the plows had carved a path, the snow now flowed like smoothed bolts of gleaming satin.

It was almost 6 P M when Jeff remembered Matt Quinby's sarcastic reference to drinks that night. Hurriedly he put on hat, gloves and scarf. It would be good to see someone else after this day of solitude, to get into a warm building and out of his coat for awhile.

It would even be good to get out in the snow again.

*

That night, Tom Casey told the press it would take two or three days more to get the federal disaster relief efforts underway because of the unanticipated wind and continuing snow

Mayor Makowski also spoke with the press, to announce that New York City Mayor Abraham Beame had offered Buffalo four huge snowblowers, complete with drivers and mechanics. They'd been scheduled to arrive earlier in the day by plane, but the continuing wind and visibility problems had made the flight impossible.

According to the mayor, private companies had called from as far away as Denver and Los Angeles to offer equipment and help.

"One of the greatest challenges of my life is right here, right now," Makowski concluded.

*

At 9 PM, William Bellis, flight operations officer for the National Guard, answered an emergency phone call at the Niagara Falls Airport restaurant. It was Dr. John Cudmore, Lieutenant Colonel of the Medical Corps, New York Army National Guard. He'd just received an urgent request from doctors at a hospital in Bradford, Pennsylvania, about 135 miles away. A five-month-old boy was in critical condition, unable to breathe without assistance. He would die, probably before morning, unless he could be flown to the special respiratory apparatus at Children's Hospital in Buffalo.

"How soon can you leave?" asked Cudmore.

"I'll call you back," Bellis told him.

Since Saturday morning Bill Bellis had been making emergency decisions. In fact, unable to dig his car out of a thirty-foot snow drift, he had requested a helicopter at the Amherst apartment complex where he lived. Hovering seventy-five feet above a narrow alley separating two buildings, the copter crew lowered a hoist and Bill, clutching a suitcase in one hand and the cable in the other, shot skyward through gusting wind at a speed of ten feet per second.

Like most of the decisions he was to make during the storm, the one to be airlifted to work was dictated by necessity. It was his job to coordinate all National Guard emergency transport from the Niagara airport, to determine what emergencies needed priority and to assign the aircraft and personnel. He'd sent copters to Fuhrmann Boulevard in search of stranded motorists that might signal from their vehicles. Others transported two kidney patients to hospitals for emergency dialysis treatment. National Guard helicopters delivered food to Tri-County Hospital in Gowanda and to Chaffee Hospital in Springville.

Flickenger's Warehouse near Como Park Boulevard had opened its doors to provide food for the needy, but access to the fa-

152

cility by road was impossible; National Guard helicopters made the pick-ups and deliveries.

Most of the flights Bellis assigned involved delivering blood, drugs and food to the ill and the stranded. In out-of-the-way places, snowmobilers converted snowbanks into helipads by driving repeatedly across an area until the snow was flat and packed. In one such case, a Guard helicopter had brought insulin to a snowbound woman who had already gone into shock and would have died without that delivery.

Still, no request had been quite as ambitious as the one made by Dr. Cudmore. Bellis hurried to his office and called the weather bureau. All over the area, he was told, there existed almost zero visibility, extreme turbulence and severe icing at higher altitudes. The Bell "Huey" chopper Bellis would use for the flight was a tough machine that needed no pampering. With a forty-eight-foot rotor, a fifty-two-foot overall length and a turbo jet engine that generated 1,250 horsepower, it would take enormous punishment. But there were certain conditions that no helicopter could handle—one was icing, another severe turbulence.

Bellis called Bradford. If anything, conditions were worse there than in Buffalo. The Bradford airport was located in a deep valley, and trying to land a plane between the mountains with no visibility was to attempt suicide.

Bellis called Dr. Cudmore at the Connecticut Street Armory.

"We're not gonna make the flight, Doc," he told him. "Conditions are impossible."

For several seconds there was no response. Then Cudmore said, "You realize, of course, that this is a life-death situation. The child might well be gone by morning."

"Yes, I understand."

"Can't you get a crew together?"

"Yes."

"Then why not take the chance?"

It was Bellis who paused. "Sir, I can't risk killing a pulmonary technician, a physician, a pilot, co-pilot and two crew members so maybe we can save one life." The doctor said nothing.

"Look," said Bellis finally, "we'll keep on it. If there's any break in the weather, I'll get back to you."

23

That night, Jeff Hensey rented a room at the Statler and had his first good night's sleep in a week. Several miles to the east, Rose Ann Wagner also slept well, having worked all day on the many chores that had accumulated while she was stranded at Emil's Inn. South of the city, Paul Dengler dreamed, as he had on several nights since the previous Wednesday, of people freezing to death on the Skyway. It was a very quiet Monday night except in the scattered locations where the National Guard, the city's Streets Sanitation Department and the scattered state and private crews continued to work.

Along the lakefront, police officers continued searching cars stranded since Friday—there had been reports of bodies in some of the vehicles. The rescuers were almost imperceptible in that vast expanse of whiteness, as though floundering in a great sea. There, virtually on the face of the lake, they were the first to notice the change.

The gusts came with suddenness and violence, hurling the snow crystals like tiny darts in horizontal sheets across the landscape. The wind raced at fifty miles per hour across the whole breadth of the city, shaking the windows at the Salvation Army Headquarters on Main Street, sweeping clear the roof at Chef's Restaurant and the Seneca Street Garage. Like a sandblaster, the snow crystals smoothed the charred juttings of former houses on Whitney Place, pelted the huddled rumps of bison at the zoo.

In the wind's howl was a new ferocity, and the sound awakened many. Jeff Hensey rolled over to gaze out the hotel room window, and saw nothing but snow.

Carl Reese, the police officer who had walked to Emergency Hospital Saturday morning to bring insulin to the pregnant woman at Chef's Restaurant, heard the wind, too. He'd been awake all night hoping the medication his doctor had prescribed for indigestion would bring some relief. But the pain had continued, and now, at 5 A.M., he was trying to rest on the living room sofa. Like many officers, he'd put in a long weekend—from Friday morning till 2 P.M. Saturday, and all day Sunday. Monday had been his day off, but he couldn't rest because of the pain. For forty-five minutes, he lay listening to the snow crystals drive against the window. Then the pain increased and he gasped. At about 6:45 A.M., Carl Reese died of a heart attack.

*

All night, William Bellis had monitored weather reports. Neither New York Central nor Cleveland indicated any likelihood of changing weather patterns. Bradford continued to experience violent winds and ice. Bellis had but to look out his window to realize that conditions hadn't changed in Buffalo, either.

If the chopper could keep close to the ground, he thought, the icing would be minimal. But with poor visibility, and especially at night, he could give no thought to such a risk. The only alternative was high altitude, where the wind could not hurl the copter into an unseen hillside or electric power line, but to consider that he'd need a clear picture of weather conditions in the upper atmosphere between Buffalo and Bradford. He sent a radio message to all airlines that might be in the area.

An American Airlines pilot responded. He said he was flying from New York to Chicago and offered to deviate from his flight plan to pass over Bradford. A short while later, he radioed Bellis: Even his commercial airliner was taking a beating in those winds, and icing up.

At 4:15 A.M., Bellis called Dr. Cudmore and learned that the boy was still alive. The weather conditions hadn't improved, but an hour and a half would bring dawn, and there was a chance that, flying fifty feet above the ground, ten feet above the trees, taking it with extreme caution, they might reach Bradford. Bellis told Cudmore to alert the pulmonary therapist and other medical personnel at Children's Hospital. Then he assigned a flight crew with Joe Chapados as pilot.

Bellis himself would go along, not only to take over the piloting when Chapados needed a break, but for the more important reason that he alone knew the route to Bradford perfectly. For some years, he'd made the flight regularly for the gas company, inspecting a pipeline that ran from Buffalo to Bradford. In daylight, the pipe would probably be visible from fifty feet up, and they would simply follow it.

Shortly after 6 A.M., the copter started south. Already, the snow had melted and frozen on the windshield, making forward visibility impossible. But the draft kept the snow away from the clear plastic panel at their feet, and it was through this that Bellis and Chapados viewed the world outside the copter. When an occasional squall brought a complete whiteout, Chapados immediately stopped their forward movement, hovering, rising slowly to avoid being tossed into the trees. But the whiteouts were rare, and usually the clearing where the pipe lay, if not the pipe itself, could be seen through the floor panel.

They had covered about half the distance when a small creek flashed beneath the helicopter.

"Hold it," Bellis said. "There's a high-tension power line about a hundred feet ahead."

"Great. We're never gonna find the wires in this weather."

"We'll look for the stanchions."

Slowly Chapados raised the copter while Bellis peered through the floor panels.

"Move left a little," he said. "You better climb a little more."

A moment later: "All right, I see it." The vague outline of the tower reached out of the snow a safe distance below. Chapados continued forward, dropped the copter lower, found the pipeline and continued south.

It was still early morning when the helicopter landed at the helipad of Bradford Hospital. In moments, it was back in the air carrying the infant north to Buffalo.

Increased wind and snow made the return flight more difficult, and Bellis, now at the controls, twice decided to make a forced landing. Each time, visibility improved sufficiently for him to continue the flight, and by midmorning the big "Huey" touched down on the parking ramp of Children's Hospital.

That afternoon Bellis, still coordinating flights and determining emergency priorities, took a moment to call Dr. Cudmore.

"The boy's doing well," said the physician. "He'll survive."

*

That morning, the Buffalo post office announced there would be no mail delivery after all.

Tom Casey said he was canceling his plans to fly by helicopter over three counties to gain a more detailed picture of the storm's effect because the wind and snow made it too dangerous.

And Mayor Stanley Makowski, after conferring with Streets Commissioner James Lindner and Deputy Mayor Leslie Foschio, finally declared a state of emergency and gave police the authority, if not the order, to ticket motorists.

It was an act that James Lindner had angrily demanded. Saturday and Sunday his crews appeared to be making progress. Then a relatively few foolish motorists had tied up the streets again.

"We get the streets cleared and send a snowplow out and he finds eight cars there," Lindner's aide told the press. "The public hasn't really helped, in spite of all these pleas. People are still driving their cars." In one intersection, off Memorial Drive on the city's East Side, seventy-three cars had been abandoned.

Had the ban been put into effect Saturday, Sunday or even Monday, he said, perhaps there would have been some progress made. Now, with visibility again approaching zero and severe blowing and drifting, Lindner was almost helpless.

The three hundred troops from the Engineering Battalion at Fort Bragg, North Carolina, were scheduled to arrive at the Buffalo International Airport at 9:30 A.M., the pilot receiving hazardous duty pay for the flight. But the wind and snow proved too severe and the plane was rerouted to another city.

At the Donovan Building, one of Tom Casey's aides admitted to a reporter that there continued to be total lack of coordination between the city, county, state and federal agencies. Casey himself repeatedly answered specific questions with vague generalities and pep rally predictions: "In a week we'll see real movement, and in two weeks we'll be sweeping the streets. I'll guarantee that—if the weather holds."

Casey was, in fact, depending heavily on the Army Corps of Engineers to represent the federal government's efforts; the National Guard was nominally coordinating with the State Department of Transportation, frequently following the wisdom of its own officers in cleaning streets they recognized as essential to emergency travel and working closely with the city of Buffalo, as Governor Carey had directed.

157

But the Army Corps offered Tom Casey little comfort. Some contracts had been drawn and even signed, but the storm continued to make work almost impossible. A few private contracting crews did make an effort, but communication between personnel at the Army Corps Control Center and the crews in the field was frequently nonexistent. Corps field inspectors traveling with the crews spent hours trying to make contact with the Center for new assignments—locating a telephone near the work site became a major chore, and getting past the busy signals at the Center's overused phones proved a frequently impossible task. Even people at the Corps headquarters confronted waiting lines to make necessary outgoing calls. And there was almost as great a lack of coordination at the Corps headquarters in matching incoming calls and requests for help with the proper staff member as existed at the Donovan Building.

That morning, the mayor invited the press into his office while he placed a telephone call to President Jimmy Carter. The President wasn't available, but several hours later, Jack Watson, a Presidential aide, returned the call. Makowski told him of the city's problems:

—One-third of the fire department's pumpers and rescue-squad vehicles had broken down.

—Snow-removal equipment had deteriorated to virtual nonexistence.

—Looting was so rampant that it was damaging the morale of the citizens.

—So costly had the winter been in overtime wages and equipment repair and replacement that the city faced economic catastrophe.

"This city is fighting for its life," said the mayor, "and now we're being flooded with bills. This city is fighting for its life, and we're in a position where we can't help ourselves any longer. We need financial assistance."

What Makowski was asking for specifically was a major disaster declaration. Since Saturday, even before Tom Casey arrived in the city, state and local politicians had made every effort to have President Carter declare the Buffalo area not only a federal emergency but a "major disaster area." The difference in the two designations would amount to millions of dollars for, while the emergency provided all necessary assistance to remove snow, the major-disaster designation would make possible federal reimbursements to the city for all storm-related expenditures and losses. It would pay for the overtime required of police, fire and streets department personnel, for vehicles broken or destroyed because of the storm, for all costs the area incurred in hiring private contractors to remove snow and cars.

Even private businesses could be helped through the major disaster declaration, for they would be eligible for long-term federal loans to cover losses suffered because of the blizzard.

Watson, Carter's aide, listened patiently. Then he told the mayor that he should address his problems to Thomas Casey.

24

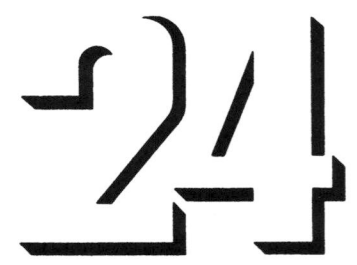

For more than six days, the great low-pressure pocket had remained stalled over the Canadian wilderness, its center hovering above James Bay, 500 miles north of Lake Erie. As air rushes to the vacuum and water flows to the whirlpool, so the west winds and the great masses of Arctic air it dragged in tow had raced across thousands of miles, and had ebbed and tumbled through an infinite number of influences to fill the great atmospheric hollow, the low pressure center. Compelled south by the earth's spinning, the wind did not plunge directly into the vacuum but skirted it, its speed increasing like that of a tornado as the circumference of its journey around the void grew smaller.

Steadily the winds came, steadily they seeped into the low-pressure pocket. Long before those six days had passed, the vacuum would have filled and the wind ceased its rushing but for the formation of other, smaller low pressure systems high above the Canadian tundra. As they came into being, each created its own wind; yet each was also tugged by the great sweep of the westerlies toward the massive low pressure system above the James Bay.

There, they united to provide new life to the system. Thus, the winds continued.

*

At the North Pole, the endless night endured, but to the south, across the fringes of the Arctic Circle, across the still ice and tundra, the sun had appeared briefly since the twenty-first of January. With every hour, its rays fell more directly across the northern hemisphere. The earth absorbed the heat hungrily; the ocean reflected it.

Over the North Atlantic, reflected heat was not lost into space but was trapped by a blanket of cloud and dissipated its warmth in the atmosphere. The process had been continuing for almost a week before that Wednesday night when Paul Dengler coaxed the green Hornet onto the Skyway.

That growing mass of warm air was one of an incalculable host of factors in the global atmosphere that, on Tuesday, February 1, 1977, stirred the vast, lazy low pressure area over James Bay. The sweeping westerlies veered toward the warm, light air above the Atlantic, and with the great wind the low pressure pocket drifted—sluggishly at first, pouring into the St. Lawrence River Valley northwest of Halifax. Then, with little diminishing of strength, it continued east into the atmosphere above the ocean.

*

Jeff Hensey noticed the change from his office window Tuesday afternoon. The sky grew rapidly brighter, the winds dropped to about twelve miles an hour and for the first time since Sunday morning he could see the city before him. A front-end loader was busy dumping snow into a truck on Niagara Street. Another crew worked on Delaware.

At the Broadway Garage, James Lindner stopped speaking in midsentence when sunlight brightened the window.

On the second floor of City Hall, Stanley Makowski viewed the clearing with unspeakable gratitude. An aide later said he saw tears on the mayor's cheeks.

Tom Casey at the Donovan Building expressed no surprise that the storm had abated—he'd already explained several times that the federal government would deal effectively with the problem.

Bill Strobele was on duty again in the radio room at police headquarters on Franklin Street and didn't know for some time that the snow had stopped. Precinct 3 had completely lost one of its cars, and Bill was busy helping to find it. All at once he remembered a call he'd taken Friday during the height of the blizzard.

"I know where that car is," he radioed to the search crew. "It's buried up there on Niagara Street. In fact, I'll tell you *right* where it is—on Niagara at Hudson, southwest side of the street."

That afternoon, Bill Strobele's two sons and many neighbors, weary of waiting for some government agency's help, shoveled open their entire block by hand.

As the sky cleared, a police helicopter spotted two snowmobiles just east of Christian Island on a desolate stretch of Ontario shoreline. Upon landing, the officers discovered two men and two children, nine and twelve, huddling together in a small hole they'd dug in a snowdrift. They'd been stranded since Saturday morning, when they'd dug a snow cave, and built a small fire in front of it. They'd survived with no great discomfort.

With the clearing weather, snow-removal efforts picked up. The plane carrying the troops from Fort Bragg finally arrived, and many were put to work with shovels. Among those who had faced continuing frustration in their efforts to clean the streets there now spread a sense of heady victory, and they hurled themselves to the task like a rallying football team.

The enthusiasm produced some predictable side effects. Near Camp Drum, a fifty-two-ton Marine personnel carrier, speeding to a work location, flattened a State Police car buried under five and a half feet of snow. An Army carrier did the same to a car that was occupied, although no one was hurt.

Buried cars were frequently damaged or destroyed, and one reporter asked a rotary plow driver if he wasn't concerned about that. He answered that he didn't mind hitting small cars: "Volkswagens are okay—they go right through the rotary blades."

Lou Vallone, who had hauled snow for the National Guard since Sunday night, was stalled again Tuesday under circumstances that had grown intensely frustrating by their frequency. Vallone's was the third and final truck in a convoy removing snow from an important side street. Guardsmen with bullhorns had announced the clearing effort on that particular block several times, and had knocked on doors asking that all cars be moved to nearby previously cleared locations. All the neighbors had cooperated except one—a single car continued to partially block the street for more than an hour. The owner refused to move it, and the dump trucks couldn't pass.

Then, without warning, the first truck lurched forward. There was a resounding snap as the car's mirror broke off and landed in the snow.

The second driver revved up the engine, shifted into gear, paused, then let out the clutch. With a piercing screech, a sharp edge of the truck's body tore a gash along the length of the car. Half a block away, Guardsmen turned to see what had happened.

Now it was Lou Vallone's turn, and he revved the engine with satisfaction. All along, removing the snow had been the basic problem, but the snow was an uncontrollable factor, fate. These cars, on the other hand, had compounded the snow's effects—and that was not fate. It was something people, cooperating, could have prevented. The car was the symbol of the enemy, and Lou Vallone prepared for war.

The door of the house before which the car was parked flew open and a middle-aged man hurried down the steps, still tugging on his coat. Pointing a demanding finger at Lou, he hurried to the car, studied the damage, cast a furious gaze at Lou and climbed into the vehicle. A moment later he was backing it down the street.

The Guard's military orientation prompted it to get the job done in blitz fashion—quickly, thoroughly and without undue concern for side effects. Thus, the huge scoop buckets chomped into a number of buried cars and uprooted a few fire hydrants. One loader operator, digging into a pile of snow, came up with the neatly detached front end of a Lincoln Continental.

Among the Army Corp's private contractors, too, were those who implemented a philosophy of victory at any cost. Two teenagers who had come from Pennsylvania in a tow truck set the record for removing cars from streets to allow the plows through. Their method was to hook their chain to the most readily available part of the car—axle, door frame, fender or bumper—and pull. Frequently, they dragged cars sideways along the narrow roads, paying no heed to the thumps and crashes as the vehicles bounced off of other parked cars.

*

Optimism spread quickly as, throughout Buffalo and most of western New York, the population could see busy snow removal crews. Once again people grew restless and impatient to travel, and only the traffic bans kept motorists off the streets.

Tuesday night, ignoring the ban, Jeff persuaded a mechanic to meet him at the garage, and in half an hour they had the Oldsmobile started. By then, the streets were clear to South Park, and with the traffic ban in effect, there were few other motorists to contend with. It was not until he reached the intersection at Abbott that a police officer stopped him and issued the citation he'd anticipated, and he accepted with a polite nod. He wouldn't even contest it, he decided—it was worth the price to get home again.

25

Almost no snow fell on Wednesday, and occasionally during the day the sun broke through the clouds. People turned to the sky with open smiles.

An army of machinery and personnel descended upon the city. At three o'clock that morning, Mayor Makowski met eleven men and seventy-five tons of equipment at the Niagara Falls Airport. Flown in from New York City on a U.S. Air Force 3-5A, the world's largest transport, were four snowblowers, a scoop loader, two cars and a truck, and it took that arsenal only ninety minutes to plow the twenty miles to Buffalo. By dawn, the New York City force was attacking Fuhrmann Boulevard, on its way to freeing dozens of workers who had been trapped at the Freezer Queen plant since Friday. Several workers preceded the heavy equipment on foot, jabbing poles through the snow in search of buried automobiles.

By then, the National Guard had put 612 troops into action, many of them with shovels. Another 300 troops flew in from Fort Bragg along with six four-wheel drive trucks brought from Rochester to help the Postal Service deliver mail.

A crew of Army helicopter pilots arrived from Massachusetts and spent ten days at the Executive Hotel before returning home. They were given no assignments because at any moment another sudden squall might occur, a complete whiteout, and under such conditions any pilot unfamiliar with the city might crash.

That morning, the Army Corps of Engineers put twenty-four private contractors to work in Erie County and eight more in sur-

164

rounding areas. In all, they operated forty-eight front loaders, thirty-two dump trucks and four plows.

An Air Force plane from Pittsburgh delivered 490 cots and 400 blankets. Another from Cleveland brought blades and repair parts for James Lindner's broken-down equipment.

With food supplies running low even at the warehouses, massive supplies of fresh foods would soon be needed, and that required getting the railroad lines opened again. About seventy U.S. Marines were given the task.

Mayor Makowski was something of a hero on Wednesday, for it was generally agreed that the ban on traffic was as important as the moderating weather in permitting the snow crews to work effectively. Violators of the ban faced possible five-hundred-dollar fines and ninety-day jail sentences, sufficient to prompt most people to walk or take buses to stores and jobs. Only ninety-seven people were ticketed for illegal driving.

Said the mayor in a press conference: "I want to lift the ban on driving as soon as possible, but once you lift that ban you'll have too many vehicles stymieing the work that's going on."

In the course of the day, many major roads were cleared curb to curb—South Park, Delaware and Tupper among them. Heavy equipment dug through fifteen-foot drifts to the end of Fuhrmann Boulevard and the Coast Guard base there to free the twenty-eight personnel stranded for seven days, since the night of January 27, when the squall had trapped Paul Dengler and Jeff Hensey on the Skyway.

A report from Watertown, northeast of Buffalo, announced that Interstate 81 had finally been opened to allow 1,800 stranded persons, many of them Canadians headed for a Florida vacation, to leave the area.

*

Rescues occurred everywhere—except, as state and local officials continued to complain, at City Hall. The storm had hurled Buffalo into financial chaos; only a Presidential disaster declaration could save it, they said.

Federal Disaster Assistance Administrator coordinator Tom Casey was the one man who blocked access to untold millions of dollars, for President Jimmy Carter, who with the stroke of a pen could make the declaration, had responded to each plea in the same way: He had told New York Governor Hugh Carey and Congressman Jack Kemp on Saturday, Senator Daniel P. Moynihan on Monday and

Mayor Makowski and County Executive Ed Regan on Tuesday—all through aides—that he awaited a recommendation from Tom Casey. The pressure on Casey became enormous, but he had faced the same many times in his career under seven Presidents. "I'm neither for nor against a major disaster declaration," he said. "If the state can work up the justification for it, I'll consider it." Until then, until he was convinced that the area required more aid to deal with the storm's effect than the federal government could provide through the simple emergency declaration, Casey would not yield. It was not his responsibility to help bail out an economy that had been ailing before the winter began, nor to replace snow removal equipment that had been inadequate long before the blizzard. The federal government's commitment was simply to offset to some extent the crippling effects of the blizzard.

Thus, new storm clouds gathered over City Hall, the Rath Building and the Donovan Building.

Wednesday evening Steve Weller, writing in his column "Typewriter Ribbin'," expressed an opinion of increasing popularity: "I for one feel the current incessant chatter about wind chill factors and clogged streets betrays shallow minds and a depressingly narrow range of interest."

*

Late Wednesday night, Congress passed the Emergency Natural Gas Act giving the President the power to declare a natural gas emergency and order gas moved from state to state when life and property are threatened. President Carter signed it into law immediately and ordered that gas supplies be piped promptly from California, South Texas and the Pacific Northwest to the Eastern Seaboard. It would be a slow journey, however, for gas moves through pipelines at only fifteen miles an hour.

At the same time, Carter declared the state of Ohio a disaster area. Both Columbia Gas and Dayton Power and Light had imposed a virtually 100 percent curtailment on gas use to large commercial and industrial customers.

26

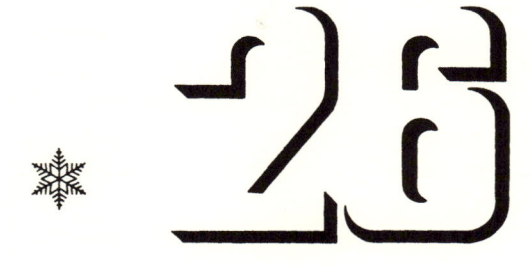

Thursday morning, the city awakened to discover that Mayor Makowski had lifted the travel ban and stores, factories and offices would be open for business as usual. Thomas Casey learned the news that morning when, during his daily briefing with representatives of the various agencies, someone handed him a copy of the *Courier-Express*. He read a few paragraphs, turned a violent red and threw the paper across the office with expletives that caused the Salvation Army liaison to blush.

The news produced general astonishment outside of City Hall, for the administration had neither advised nor consulted state or federal officials before acting. Casey had specifically excluded city representatives from all briefing and coordination meetings, so the city had acted alone.

The mayor's decision might well have been anticipated. He had refused to impose a traffic ban all winter in spite of monumental traffic tie-ups, abandoned cars and uncleared roads because the local business community had opposed it, and now, after a week during which the economy had been frozen to a standstill, the outcry from a few powerful members of the business community against the day-old traffic ban constituted, in the mayor's own words, "enormous pressure." He'd been "besieged by requests, indeed demands, from many major commercial and industrial firms to lift the driving ban so that those major employers could move toward resuming normal operations."

The presidents of large companies had insisted they were on

167

the verge of losing major contracts. Smaller companies promised they'd go bankrupt. Still others threatened to move out of the city. Even union representatives told the mayor the ban would leave thousands of workers in economic ruin.

Calling a press conference, the mayor said, "I was impressed with what they told me. If these firms close down or leave town and take their jobs with them, the damage is permanent. Long after this storm has become a dim memory, people will still only remember that the mayor's driving ban cost them their jobs."

So, with the approval of all his advisors and aides except James Lindner and transportation commissioner Dan Hoyt, the mayor lifted the ban. In doing so, he gave no thought to a prediction from the National Weather Service at the Buffalo International Airport. The forecast for Thursday was for snow.

It was as though the city had lapsed into a time warp Thursday morning. Countless thousands, like the mayor the night before, like the entire city nine days earlier, paid no heed to the forecast, but climbed into their automobiles and swarmed downtown. Upon reaching center city, they discovered that most parking lots were unplowed, so thousands left their cars on the streets, narrowing most four-lane arteries to two lanes of stalled or creeping traffic.

The snow began falling before most people were out of bed Thursday morning, increasing under a brisk breeze during the rush hour and reaching its heaviest density between two o'clock and five that afternoon. By then, cars were once again scattered everywhere, traffic jams were monumental and snow-removal efforts were again at a standstill.

The public, almost to a person, responded in anger when asked about the lifting of the ban. "That guy Makowski's inept, a fool, and probably out of his goddamn mind!" exclaimed one irate driver. Said another, "Makowski ought to leave town on the next gust of wind." She, too, had driven downtown that morning to go shopping.

A bus driver had another perspective, however: "Look, nobody put a gun to their heads and told 'em they hada come drivin' to town—they had the same facts as Makowski. If he made a mistake, what about them stupid bastards that got stuck? Just always blame the other guy."

While the mayor's decision stalled snow-removal efforts in Buffalo, the new storm closed roads throughout western New York. Squalls and heavy drifting combined with near-zero visibility to produce conditions that officials in some areas claimed were even more severe than those of the previous Friday. States of emergency continued or were newly declared in the towns of Alden, Brant, Evans, Lancaster, Newstead, North Collins and Wales, among others. Many roads in southern Erie County were reported blown shut during the day. The same was true of Niagara, Chautauqua and Wyoming counties.

And in the heart of Buffalo, more than 100 cars were still stranded on Fuhrmann Boulevard.

Like the frayed remnants of a broken army, James Lindner's crews drove their equipment out of the Broadway Garage to the same streets they'd cleared more times that winter than anyone could remember. Among them, none thought in terms of a victory; few even hoped to hold the roads, keeping them open at least for emergency travel. The move was one of concerted despair. Yet, for no reason they understood, most of the men, like soldiers fighting a hopeless battle for a noble cause, worked that day with the same determination they'd displayed when, four months earlier, the first snowflakes of the season had fallen on the city.

Elsewhere in the county, the National Guard, in their open-cab loaders and unheated trucks, attacked the roads that, in some towns, were still closed border to border. In Buffalo, the Guard again cleared access roads to the city's hospitals, as it had daily since Sunday.

Every county had its highway crews on the roads, in spite of the heavy, blowing snow. Department of Transportation workers struggled to keep the thruway and other state roads open, and dozens of private contractors hired by the Army Corps continued at work.

That afternoon, the Red Bessie, the Salvation Army canteen, finally got some assistance. Two more canteens arrived from New York City, and were immediately put to work delivering food and hot beverages to the snow-removal crews. By then, what one Salvation Army worker referred to as a minor miracle had taken place, and it made possible extremely effective coordination between headquarters and canteen drivers.

Earlier in the week, Dave Struell, emergency coordinator for the American Radio Relay League, grew puzzled that the Salvation Army's ham-radio system, which he'd helped establish years earlier, was not broadcasting during the blizzard. Finally, he called the Main Street headquarters to learn that the equipment had been stolen. That same day, he and fellow members of the League set up new equipment on loan to the Salvation Army. When they learned that the canteens were about to be sent into the field, ham operators volunteered to go along. Thus, as headquarters workers received service requests, they radioed them to the nearest canteen. The canteens could also be in immediate contact with headquarters. Eventually, the Salvation Army had nine canteens on Buffalo area roads, each with its own ham radio operator.

The Salvation Army, Red Cross and similar groups continued answering calls Thursday from many people who had been snowbound in their homes for more than a week and desperately needed food. The TOPS Supermarket chain, learning of the problem, donated 7,000 loaves of bread to the service agencies, and, along with other staples, the bread was promptly distributed.

Late that afternoon, in response to the universal clamor against his lifting the traffic ban, Mayor Makowski announced that he would put it into effect again at midnight. Thus, the mayor became the target of universal frustration and anger—those who by driving had created a traffic problem which made travel almost impossible castigated him; those who had opposed the ban in the first place and had succeeded in having it lifted were now doubly furious. Some said Mayor Makowski decided that day not to seek re-election.

Makowski was not alone on the firing line. At the Donovan Building, Tom Casey staggered under enormously increased pressure to recommend a major disaster declaration for western New York. Earlier, the President had signed such a declaration for Florida, and, although Casey had explained the vastly different circumstances between the Buffalo and Florida situations, the pressure increased by the hour.

Even religious leaders sent a telegram to Carter urging the disaster declaration.

Casey explained that it was not a decision to be made lightly, that it would require a good deal of research to determine the number of people who had lost housing or jobs and could not get work because of the storm, the degree to which food stamps, unemployment compensation and such would be required, how much debris would need clearing once the snow was removed, the extent to which roads, bridges and streets needed replacing or repair. Those were the sort of benefits provided by the disaster declaration as compared to the emergency under which he was empowered to act, and Tom Casey was still not convinced that such remedies were needed. First, Casey wanted to clean up the streets and get the economy moving again. Then, he'd gladly study the arguments for the disaster declaration. And if they were persuasive, he'd make the recommendation to the President.

What Tom Casey apparently didn't know at the time was that politics had already begun to brush aside his stubborn efforts to appropriate federal money prudently. Like children who through ceaseless nagging finally get their way, local, state and federal politicians continually badgered the White House, and on Thursday, the President announced that he would send his twenty-six-year-old son Chip on Friday to survey the area and bring back a special report. By then, the President had already made the crucial decision—he would not await the recommendation of his career disaster coordinator, Thomas Casey, who had been on the scene since Sunday and was one of the most experienced men in the country regarding such matters, but would make the politically expedient move of signing the disaster declaration.

But the President wasn't lacking in political acumen; he would send his own son to the area, so that the decision to send millions of federal dollars to western New York would result only incidentally from the urging of the mayor, the county executive, the governor, the senators and representatives in the Congress. Carter's son would make the recommendation that Carter would approve.

Ray Herman, writer for the *Courier-Express*, took a critical view of the whole thing. " 'What's "Chip" Carter going to do here, shovel snow?' " he quoted a Buffalo political leader.

It was to be a gala occasion, according to Herman: "Also scheduled to be on hand to exhibit some compassion are New York's two U.S. senators, Democrat Daniel P. Moynihan and Republican Jacob K. Javits; Margaret 'Midge' Costanza, the former vice mayor of Rochester and now a special counsel to Carter; and an aide to Jack Watson, also a special counsel to the President."

Pointing out that no one at the White House seemed to know what "Chip" and "Midge" were going to do in Buffalo, Herman concluded, "In recent days, the national media has descended on the Buffalo area to cover the historic snowstorm. This fact has not been lost on the politicians."

Recognizing a lost cause when he saw one, Tom Casey told the press late Thursday that he might consider making the disaster recommendation sooner than he had anticipated.

Thursday ended with both good news and bad. Buffalo fire fighters were elated to receive a dozen "mini-pumpers" on loan, along with their crews, from seven New York State counties. Not only did they replace the city's own pumpers—some of which were still frozen in the ice on Whitney Place, others broken down in various parts of the city—but, small of size and with four-wheel drive, they were capable of navigating roads that were impassable by the city's larger vehicles.

The Police Department also had good news: As the number of four-wheel drives made available to the department had increased, the police had become more effective in capturing and arresting looters until, by Thursday, such crimes fell to normal levels. To some police officers who had spent frigid hours ticketing illegally parked and abandoned cars, however, it was not such good news to learn that the city had cancelled all the tickets, along with the towing fees. Since 2,632 tickets at $12.00 each and 500 towings at $25.00 each were involved, the city thus discarded almost $50,000 in revenue.

*

The large outdoor thermometer on the Western New York Savings Bank on Lafayette Square that night announced to a handful of snow-blown pedestrians a temperature of 110 degrees. In fact, according to the Weather Bureau, a low-pressure system north of Lake Superior was expected to cross western New York by Friday night, driving temperatures back to lows of five to ten on Saturday through Monday with periods of new snow.

Another storm had formed over the Southwest on Wednesday, dumping snow over New Mexico and Colorado, then moving into the western Great Lakes region. That storm, too, could hit Buffalo on the weekend. Although no one was predicting a blizzard yet, there would certainly be squalls, and winds up to forty miles an hour.

*

By Friday morning, the National Weather Service had become more specific in its weekend weather forecast, and the news wasn't good: A storm would strike early Saturday, bringing perhaps three inches of snow, high temperatures in the teens, strong winds and a windchill factor as low as minus 50 degrees. Some snow would continue to fall every day at least until Tuesday, along with continuing subfreezing temperatures.

Because of the ban and the storm forecast, downtown stores announced they would remain closed Friday and on the weekend.

The Winter Carnival, originally scheduled for January 23–24, then postponed to January 29–30, then until February 5–6, was postponed again until February 12–13.

*

At midmorning, twenty-six-year-old James Carter III, the President's son, arrived at Buffalo International Airport with the anticipated cast of politicians, local, state and federal. Only Erie County Executive Edward Regan, in the forefront of the battle to rescue Erie County from the blizzard's ravages, was not invited. He was a Republican.

Mayor Makowski greeted the President's son, escorting him to the first limousine in a cavalcade of official and press cars, and the two-hour, thirty-five-mile fact-gathering tour began.

Local officials had planned a route through Erie and Niagara counties that would leave young Carter in no doubt that a disaster had indeed struck the area. But Mayor Makowski had prayed daily for clear weather and, although the ominous threat of another blizzard lingered less than twenty-four hours away, a bright sun beamed from a blue sky. Snow-swept fields appeared serene and by-standers greeted the cavalcade with smiles.

The route along which the cars moved had been cleared curb to curb. All over the area men were working to dig out—4,000 of them operating 500 machines—12 snowblowers, 155 front-end loaders, 181 dump trucks, 28 plows and 124 other pieces of equipment. While Carter and his entourage toured, Buffalo's buses were running close to schedule again, and airlines were flying regular routes.

To get a feel of the situation from the people themselves, young Carter stopped to chat with one surprised woman and a few children, and the conversation was photographed and duly reported by a bevy of journalists.

Finally, Carter made his last stop before returning to the airport. He climbed to the top of a huge drift that had been preserved on Fuhrmann Boulevard to tell reporters, "I plan to talk with Dad across the dinner table and in a formal report—but there's more data needed and coming in."

A few hours later, Carter's plane landed in Washington. During the flight home, Senators Jacob K. Javits and Daniel P. Moynihan had composed a five-page letter urging the President to declare nine western and northern New York counties national disaster areas. They had the letter delivered immediately to the President—with copies to the press.

A few hours later—presumably after dinner—President Carter allowed a White House aide to telephone Democratic representative Henry J. Nowak of Buffalo with the news that Carter would sign the disaster declaration Saturday morning.

*

Since a small uproar had greeted the Makowski administration announcement of amnesty for all whose cars had been towed or ticketed during the blizzard, another announcement was made Friday by the city's transportation commissioner, Daniel W. Hoyt. He explained that the decision with regard to the twenty-five-dollar towing fee was still to be made. Regarding questions concerning the previous day's announcement, he said, "The information as of yesterday was correct. Perhaps we've changed our minds."

27

So there would be still another stand. Like the fisherman in *The Old Man and the Sea*, Lindner prepared for yet another encounter. Five months of snow and Arctic air, and yet the winter, like an invincible general, would hurl fresh troops from a limitless army against the city. For five months, Lindner had repulsed the attacks. His troops were in disarray, his weapons broken. Yet he continued, not with the fisherman's stoic doggedness, but with anger.

The city was ready. For the first time that winter, Lindner knew that he had enough equipment and men available to sweep the streets clear even in the most violent storm except during zero visibility, when no one would be driving anyway. This time they would break the seige. That Friday night, the week-long warming trend in the Arctic continued. Great slabs of ice fractured with resounding cracks; the sheer, gleaming faces of glaciers tumbled into the sea with a roar.

Across the Northern Hemisphere, the extremes of cold and warm continued to mellow, the gradients of high and low pressure to moderate, the furious soaring and plunging of hot and cold air to abate. The westerlies leaped less deeply into the Polar regions, and on that Friday night, February 4, they did not rush as far south. In fact, their path that night began to resemble their usual course.

It was in the tug of the westerlies that the Chicago storm moved east toward Lake Erie, where it fell under the influence of another of the low pressure masses that had formed in the James Bay area with oppressive regularity all winter. Attracted to the low pressure pocket, the storm would descend directly upon Buffalo with enormous violence.

That night, however, the anticipated low pressure pocket failed to develop at the James Bay. While western New York awaited the storm, the westerlies carried it southeast across Long Island, then north to Connecticut and Rhode Island before rushing out to sea.

*

The National Weather Service, attacked a week earlier for not cautiously predicting a blizzard when one was possible, was attacked again for predicting a storm that didn't materialize.

*

Saturday morning, President Carter formally declared the nine counties of western and northern New York a disaster area. He also announced the federal emergency for eleven counties in Michigan said to have snow and wind problems equal to that of Buffalo.

The declaration stimulated a celebratory atmosphere, particularly among leading politicians, virtually all of whom held press conferences and issued releases detailing their role in bringing what would certainly amount to huge sums of the nation's money into the area. In addition to the Army Corps of Engineers and the Federal Disaster Assistance Administration, several other federal departments would participate in spending the funds: the departments of Agriculture; Labor; Health, Education and Welfare; Housing and Urban Development among them. Free housing would be made available for up to twelve months for those whose homes had been rendered uninhabitable. The government would pay rents and mortgages for those who claimed disaster-created hardships. Low-interest loans would be granted to businesses, farmers and individuals for necessary property repair. Farmers would be given free feed grain. Free food coupons would go to virtually anyone who asked for them. Grants of up to five thousand dollars for those who could build a case that the money was needed to recover from the disaster. Free debris removal from private as well as public land and water.

In addition, the federal government, through the disaster declaration, would repair streets, roads, bridges, water control facilities, public buildings, utilities, schools and other public facilities. Low-cost disaster loans could be made to counties, cities, towns and villages. And federal equipment and personnel would continue to be available.

Tom Casey refused to discuss the disaster designation Saturday but, under questioning, one of his aides answered curtly, "That was not his recommendation," and refused further comment. The following day, Sunday, Casey went so far as to say, "I'm encouraged about the spirit of the people. It's high, and I think the disaster declaration helped."

On Monday, however, Casey acted. The Army Corps of Engineers had hired private contractors under his authority as emergency relief coordinator. Under the new disaster declaration, Casey was not technically authorized to continue dealing directly with private contractors—instead, local government was permitted to arrange the contracts themselves and receive direct reimbursement from the federal government. Because of bureaucratic red tape, it would take about a month for the money to get to the city needing it.

On Monday, Tom Casey told the Army Corps to conclude the contracts. The city of Buffalo, financially crippled and unable to borrow money, could not afford to continue the snow removal efforts, and they ceased.

One of the most important projects that remained unfinished was the clearing of five railyards, which had been closed for more than a week, with many boxcars still loaded with food. Other trains bringing freight to the Buffalo area had been sidetracked or turned away, and finally the Association of American Railroads, at the request of the Interstate Commerce Commission, had imposed a freight embargo on the Buffalo area.

On Sunday, the Corps had sent 88 front-end loaders, 153 trucks and 9 bulldozers to the five yards, and, along with 200 temporary employees of the New York State Employment Office, they'd made some progress. On Monday, that work came to a halt.

The following day, Tuesday, Casey pulled out the Fort Bragg troops.

By Wednesday, February 9, a consortium of three of the city's major private contracting firms signed an agreement with the city to complete the snow-removal operation. Like the Army Corps, they would subcontract much of the work, using their lines of credit at local banks to pay for the work until the city received the federal funds. The contractors took nine days to complete the job.

Wednesday, February 9, constituted a turning point in the weather. Although there were traces of snow around noon, the temperature soared to 34 degrees that evening, breaking above the freezing mark for the first time in fifty-four days. The following day, it

177

reached 39, and for the rest of the week, it was in the forties. Although another foot and a half of snow fell on Buffalo during February, it melted quickly.

*

Rise up, my love, my fair one, and come away.
For, lo, the winter is past, the rain is over and gone;
The flowers appear on the earth; the singing of birds is come,
and the voice of the turtle is heard in our land.

—The Song of Solomon, 2:10

*

EPILOGUE

The Fourth Annual Erie County Winter Carnival, postponed from January 23 to 29, to February 5, then to February 12, was postponed again—until February 19–20, when it was held.

Mary Schmahl, who had won the five-thousand-dollar lottery on the night of the blizzard, won another thousand dollars in a charity raffle on February 14—two days after her father died.

Joe Falzone, the Whitney Place grocer, opened his store within a week after the fire, transporting stock by sled from delivery trucks on Niagara Street. Whitney and Virginia were closed for more than two weeks because vehicles were trapped in the ice. Shortly after the snow cleared, the city ordered Falzone to fill in the hole where his house had been.

Meteorologists for Accu-Weather, a private weather service in State College, Pennsylvania, had good personal news: Paying attention to their own forecasts of severe cold as far south as Florida, they formed a five-thousand-dollar office pool and invested in the frozen orange juice futures market. Three weeks later, they cashed in on their investment, realizing forty thousand dollars.

Less thrilled were the youth of Buffalo upon learning that school would begin again on February 14 after a two and a half week hiatus.

Downright unpleasant news reached an estimated 375 Buffalonians who, even on March 26, were still unable to locate their automobiles. According to records, most of them were not among the 7,000 towed off the streets during the storm, and were presumed stolen. The Parking Violations Bureau also had 70 cars without license plates and one hundred more that had not been claimed.

By March, Police Commissioner Thomas Blair could report that almost 40 percent of the looters operating during the blizzard had been apprehended. They had stolen about two hundred thousand dollars in goods. That figure did not include the neighborhood grocers who charged two dollars and fifty cents for a half gallon of milk because their customers couldn't make it to the supermarket, those who charged fifty dollars to plow their neighbor's tiny driveways, the hotel manager who doubled the cost of a room, the service station owner who did the same for a gallon of gas or the taxi driver who charged five people fifty dollars for a ten-minute ride.

Leslie M. Greenbaum, assistant corporate counsel for the city of Buffalo, prevented perhaps another one hundred thousand dollars in fraud. He took it upon himself to spot check the multitude of towing invoices submitted to the city by individual operators and found many cases of false billing. One ambitious but dishonest free enterpriser creating fictitious license numbers to go with the fictitious cars he claimed to tow, made the mistake of choosing a number that belonged to Greenbaum. Greenbaum insisted that he produce proof of every towing, and eventually the man was paid seventeen percent of his claims.

Perhaps the worst news came from family physicians: In March and April, abortions in Buffalo increased by forty-five percent.

The blizzard spawned an avalanche of statistics:

The Buffalo Area Chamber of Commerce reported a total economic loss to the area of $221,490,000 during the five and a half days beginning January 28. The fuel-gas curtailment added another $76,000,000 loss to the economy.

The Army Corps of Engineers had 353 of its own people working during the blizzard, hired 216 private contractors to clear snow from 3,186 miles of road in nine counties. The contractors used almost 1,000 pieces of equipment.

Buffalo firemen fought 42 fires and answered 1,570 emergency calls in the ten-day period beginning January 28.

Soon after the blizzard, the American Red Cross reported that it had distributed 5 tons of food to 84 feeding stations in western New York, feeding an estimated 50,000 people. In the first few days of the blizzard alone, the agency answered about 7,000 phone calls, with one operator handling up to 6,000 of them and accidentally disconnecting 4.

The Salvation Army fed about 67,000, distributing clothing to another 4,500 and housing 851 stranded men, women and children. More than 1,000 people volunteered to aid in the distribution efforts, which cost the Salvation Army about $75,000.

City officials finally made a firm decision regarding the 2,632 parking tickets and 500 towing charges: They waived them.

The Watertown, New York, area, including Jefferson and Lewis counties, some 150 miles northeast of Buffalo near Lake Ontario's east shore received the heaviest snowfall of the blizzard—5 feet from January 28 to February 1.

The most significant statistics were these: There were eighteen storm-related deaths in Erie County, eleven of them in Buffalo. Another five died in surrounding areas. Some suffered heart attacks while shoveling snow, a few were struck by cars or trucks. Only seven froze to death.

The Buffalo Police Department later issued 850 Certificates of Merit to those who had volunteered snowmobiles and four-wheel drives or had aided in the emergency in some other way. Thousands more who did as much, like Jeff Hensey, insisted on anonymity.

Bill Strobele, the police dispatcher, helped his mother sell her house and pack that spring. She'd spent the night of January 28 at a firehouse after the bus she was riding on stalled in a traffic jam. She was too old to spend another winter in Buffalo, she explained, and made up her mind to move to California.

National Guard pilots William Bellis and Joe Chapados, along with their helicopter crews, received the New York State Medal of Valor for their hazardous flight to Bradford, Pennsylvania. Only about fifty such awards have been issued since New York was founded.

James Lindner became a hero, at least in the eyes of the city's councilmen. During a Buffalo Common Council meeting later in the month, there was almost unanimous praise for him and his crew.

The month of March 1977 was eight degrees warmer than normal.

BIBLIOGRAPHY

Buffalo *Courier-Press*, all issues, October 1976 through February 1977.

Buffalo *Evening News*, all issues, October 1976 through February 1977.

Cornwall, Jan, *Ice Ages, Their Nature and Effects*. John Baker, Ltd., London, 1970.

Critchfield, Howard J., *General Climatology*. Prentice-Hall, Englewood Cliffs, New Jersey, 1960.

Kirk, Ruth, *Snow*. Morrow, New York, 1978.

Kurten, Bjorn, *The Ice Age*. G. P. Putnam, New York, 1972.

Ley, Willy and the editors of *Life*, *The Poles* Time Incorporated, New York, 1962.

Namias, J., "Multiple Causes of the North American Abnormal Winter of 1976–77." *Monthly Weather Review*, 106: 279–95, March 1978.

Rossi, Erno, *White Death*. 77 Publishing, Ontario, Canada, 1978.

U.S. Army, *Operation Snow Go 1977*. U.S. Army Engineers, Buffalo, New York, June 1977.

Verna, B. J., "Winter of '77." *Nuclear News*, 20:49, May 1977.

Wagner, A. J., "Weather and Circulation of January 1977." *Monthly Weather Review*, 105: 553–60, April 1977.

Woodbury, David O., *The Great White Mantle*. Viking, New York, 1962.

AUTHORS GUILD BACKINPRINT.COM EDITIONS are fiction and nonfiction works that were originally brought to the reading public by established United States publishers but have fallen out of print. The economics of traditional publishing methods force tens of thousands of works out of print each year, eventually claiming many, if not most, award-winning and one-time best-selling titles. With improvements in print-on-demand technology, authors and their estates, in cooperation with the Authors Guild, are making some of these works available again to readers in quality paperback editions. Authors Guild Backinprint.com Editions may be found at nearly all online bookstores and are also available from traditional booksellers. For further information or to purchase any Backinprint.com title please visit www.backinprint.com.

Except as noted on their copyright pages, Authors Guild Backinprint.com Editions are presented in their original form. Some authors have chosen to revise or update their works with new information. The Authors Guild is not the editor or publisher of these works and is not responsible for any of the content of these editions.

THE AUTHORS GUILD is the nation's largest society of published book authors. Since 1912 it has been the leading writers' advocate for fair compensation, effective copyright protection, and free expression. Further information is available at www.authorsguild.org.

Please direct inquiries about the Authors Guild and Backinprint.com Editions to the Authors Guild offices in New York City, or e-mail staff@backinprint.com.

Made in the USA
Lexington, KY
28 December 2010